Let's Quit Fighting About
the Holy Spirit

Peter E. Gillquist

Let's Quit Fighting About the Holy Spirit

Lakeland

LAKELAND
MARSHALL, MORGAN AND SCOTT
116 Baker Street
LONDON WIM 2BB

Copyright © 1974 by The Zondervan Corporation
First British edition 1976
ISBN 0 551 00588 2

Printed in Great Britain by
Cox & Wyman Ltd, London, Reading and Fakenham
578080R51

To the brothers and sisters in
"The Junction"
through whom I have learned there are
varieties of gifts
but the same Spirit

Contents

Preface

Because a book of this nature is open to differences of opinion, God impressed on me from the start *there is safety in a multitude of counselors* (Prov. 11:14). A number of people in His family read and commented on the manuscript and, while not mentioning all of them by name, I want to say "thank you" for their excellent suggestions. These "counselors" were all Spirit-filled Christians from a variety of backgrounds.

I suppose my good friend and college roommate, Richard Wagner of Chicago, made the classic comment of them all. As we were discussing the timeliness of the book, he remarked, "I kept on thinking as I went through the manuscript, 'I *really* hope its message will be obsolete in a year.'" My prayer is that he's right.

My thanks to Ted Anderson of Corpus Christi, and the staff and board at *Beachhead*, for allowing me use of their incomparable facilities to write most of this book. And a special word of gratitude to John and Marjorie Dold of Chicago for their willing hands which typed and duplicated the manuscript.

May I make a request? Please consider this book in its entirety, and not in isolated segments. Each chapter builds toward the next. The book is essentially *one* unit of truth, not many. Its aim is to pull together those of us who are members of Christ.

PETER E. GILLQUIST

Grand Junction, Tennessee

one / The Nature of Unity

Regardless of where you stand on the spectrum in relationship to the current outpouring of the Holy Spirit, you will most likely agree there is nothing else abroad in the church today which has caused God's people to turn on one another more than has this matter of spiritual gifts.

Oftentimes entire fellowships of believers split over disagreements on the gifts of the Spirit. Or two people who have been close in the bonds of Christ for years no longer share Him with intimacy and oneness because one of them receives a manifestation of the Spirit with which the other disagrees. It's tragic how Satan has used to *divide* us the very means God gave to unite us. The Holy Spirit was given to the body of Christ to make us one.

To Speak, or Not to Speak: That Is the Question!

A girl in her early twenties, a fairly new Christian, made application not long ago to work with a Christian organization. During the interview she was asked, "What is your feeling about tongues?"

"About what?" she asked.

"Tongues," replied the examiner.

"I don't believe I've ever heard of it," the girl said honestly. "What is tongues?"

"Well, it's a phenomenon that happened first on the day of Pentecost in Acts chapter two, where the Christians were filled with the Spirit and given the ability to utter words in languages which they had never learned. It's also referred to some in the gospels, but primarily in the Book of Acts and in First Corinthians. The reason we ask this question is because of all the trouble abroad over the matter."

"Well," said the applicant, thinking back to the original question, "if it's in the Bible, I'd have to say I agree with it. One thing I've learned since meeting Jesus Christ as my Savior is that I can depend on God's Word."

"Our policy," said the interviewer, "is that those who join our staff must first agree not to speak in tongues."

"Why, when it's in the Bible?" the girl asked.

"Well, you see, it's. . . ."

And so the conversation went. Application rejected.

On the other side of the ledger, another friend, a man aglow with the Spirit, was asked to teach the Scriptures periodically to large fellowships of Christians who believed in the gifts of the Holy Spirit and practiced them. Whenever he taught, people came by the droves to listen because of the clarity and authority he exhibited as he presented God's Word. Believers were growing steadily in the Lord, and many new people were being reached for Christ.

But then the word got out that, although this man believed wholeheartedly in the full work of the Holy Spirit, he had never experienced the manifestation of tongues.

That was it. No more teaching sessions were ever scheduled for the brother.

And all God's people said... *Why?*

SIGNS OF PROGRESS

Not long ago I was having lunch at the Billy Graham headquarters in Minneapolis with several members of the office staff. The conversation turned toward God's healing power. Two of the men related how they had been involved in seeing God miraculously heal people they knew and loved. We were all encouraged greatly by these fascinating reports. And laughter came spontaneously as the comment was made, "Isn't it ironic that we're sitting here at the Graham headquarters praising the Lord for 'faith healings,' while Oral Roberts is spending an increased amount of time on Sunday television discussing personal salvation!"

You know, I'm finding more and more that God's people are coming back to openness in the Spirit. Personal persuasions notwithstanding, believers are beginning to say, "There's got to be more happening in the kingdom of God to occupy our attention than strife. If we've got some fight within us, for heaven's sake let's stand together and aim our artillery against the domain of darkness instead of wasting our zeal on tearing each other apart."

UNITY AND COMPROMISE

But the thing which holds many of us back is, we don't want to compromise. We've experienced something of the Lord, or we've learned some truths from His Word, and we can't just up and forget it. It's become a part of us. We really *do* want oneness; we want unity in the body. But what about the matter of being true to ourselves?

I was in the Pacific Northwest recently and was met there by a close friend in Christ who was on his way through town enroute to Alaska. My purpose in being there was to speak to a Christian group, and I wanted them to meet Robin. I introduced him to these people.

13

"He's passing through here tonight," I said, "on his way to King Salmon, Alaska, where he serves a radar installation as an officer in the Air Force. He was commissioned as a second lieutenant when he graduated from college a year ago, and served last year down in Texas."

Then, turning to my friend, I said, "Rob, why don't you take a few minutes and relate to these people how you came to know Jesus Christ? And maybe tell them some of the things you have seen the Lord doing as you've served in the Air Force." Rob caught it right away, but I had completely forgotten — we were with a group of people who were pacifists, who sincerely felt a commitment to Christ carried with it an abstinence from military service. And here I'd gone and introduced him with Air Force credentials!

In the love and transparency which only the Holy Spirit can produce, my brother told of his walk with Christ and related a couple of incidents where some men had gotten turned on to the Lord at the base in Texas.

Back at our motel later that evening, Robin filled me in on my *faux pas.* I felt like a heel! If there was one specific truth the Lord had been teaching me of late, it was this matter of not putting a stumbling block in the path of other people. I expressed my apologies to Robin and asked him what he thought I should do in relationship to the group.

"I don't think you'll need to do much of anything," he said. "It was really a beautiful thing. After I'd finished talking, a guy took me aside to apologize to *me.* He told me that after you introduced me, he decided when I was finished with what I had to say he would take me aside and lay the pacifist deal on me. But instead, he came up and said he was sorry for not just accepting me as a brother in Jesus Christ, and he told me he loved me in the Lord."

Robin and I talked until late that night about the impact of this man's remarks. I thought about a number of times when, if a similar stance had been taken among Christians, ugly disputes could have been avoided. Then I recalled times when *I* should have stood for oneness in the Spirit —

14

and didn't. We agreed as we talked that if an attitude like this could sweep through the body of Christ during the next few years, there was no telling how powerfully the Spirit of God could bring His people together.

Sometimes, I suppose, we see *unity* and *compromise* as synonymous. They aren't. I seriously doubt the brother who approached Robin that evening has moved an inch with regard to his feelings about Christians taking part in military service. And I know Robin is still in the Air Force. These two men did not compromise their beliefs one iota. But they are one in Jesus Christ. They are together as can be on the Lordship of Christ; they hold difference convictions in at least one area as to what that Lordship means.

An important characteristic of Christian unity is that *ultimately* both of the people (or factions) involved in a disagreement must express love to pull it off. Otherwise, at best, it's peaceful coexistence. But fortunately, unity can *begin* with just one and have a strong chance for success.

And in Christ, we have a tremendous advantage. We are *already* one. It's our natural state as believers. This explains why Paul tells us to "preserve the unity of the Spirit in the bond of peace" (Eph. 4:3).

The Task at Hand

The Reformation pulled us out of the *theological* death of the Dark Ages. Doctrinally, some very crooked places were made straight. Could it be that the current work of the Holy Spirit will enhance the task of saving us from the *experiential* deadness of the Dark Ages — from which we never really emerged at Reformation time?

I cannot help but believe the last great job Jesus Christ wants to accomplish with His people is to bring them together as a functioning unit. In fact, Paul predicts something like this in Ephesians 5:27. He says Jesus will "present to Himself the church in all her glory, having no spot or wrinkle or any such thing; but that she should be holy and blameless."

15

Jesus Christ will not be coming back to claim an ugly bickering bride! He wants something holy, spotless. His prayer for the church was "that they may all be one" (John 17:21). Thus He has a job on His hands, and He is in the process right now of getting on with it. We are living in the age when the coming together of the body of Christ is the major theme. And the work has begun.

And to bring about awakening and unity in the body of Christ, God pours His Spirit upon men. He has done it before. He is doing it now.

AN OVERVIEW OF THIS BOOK

You will probably not agree with everything I say in the pages that follow. I am almost positive you will agree with my conclusion, but you may not line up with everything along the way — and that's great. Because what we are after here is coming together in the Lord Jesus Christ, and not to undiversify the work the Holy Spirit has done in our midst.

And I make you a promise. I am not going to put you into any kind of religious trap. No side or faction or individual will emerge victorious. The winner's circle is reserved for Christ and the whole company of His followers.

In the next three chapters I will consider why sectarian attitudes of "we got it and you don't" get started. For some, these chapters will be more educational than they will be inspirational. It may well be there are sections you wish to skim. But I feel a general understanding of why factions in the body of Christ occur is important, so we may in the future avoid them.

The later chapters will report on some of the exciting things God is doing with His people at this hour. We will relate these happenings to the concepts of love and oneness among believers, for which we all yearn.

We are dealing here with the most crucial problem facing the body of Christ in this entire century. If you have been familiar with the debate over the baptism of the Holy Spirit, tongues, and other charismatic manifestations, you will know whereof I speak. If your exposure to the tension in the church over the work of the Holy Spirit has been limited, then reserve a place "on the back burner" for what is being said. For this division is a device of the adversary which can be swept under the rug no longer.

two / The Nature of Division

Now concerning spiritual gifts, brethren, I do not want
you to be unaware. (I Corinthians 12:1)

For years we who have known the Lord Jesus Christ have
asked God for an awakening among His people. We have
told Him that we have hungered to see the world confronted with the Gospel; that we truly desired a genuine
outpouring of His Holy Spirit.

Almost as far back as I can recall since becoming a Christian, I have all but assaulted the Lord with a request for
awakening. I read books containing the history of great revivals, and I wanted to see a real revival — whatever it was
like — in my day. I'm sure not all my motivation was spiritual — I just wanted to be around when God did something
big and powerful — but I'll tell you that most of those mo-

18

tives were right. I wanted, and still do want, to see men and nations turn to Jesus Christ.

SLEEPERS, AWAKE!

Well, then it began to happen. What hundreds of thousands of Christians from all backgrounds had prayed for began to happen. It was an awakening tailor-made for our day, for our culture, to meet our problems. It started somewhere in the late forties and began booming in the sixties. *God began to pour out His Holy Spirit!*

The secular press calls the most recent surge the Jesus Movement, and certainly the Jesus Movement was part of it. But it wasn't just with the kids. Big folks started coming alive, too. The charismatic movement took on steam. Upheavals came in the organized church. The very look and stance of the body of Christ began to change.

People became bolder, more vocal. Folks had the courage to come right out and admit that they loved Jesus Christ, even through such strange media as bumper stickers and banners. Grown men who five years before wouldn't have been seen dead doing it now actually stepped up and hugged brothers in the Lord whom they hadn't seen for a while.

But when God really started to pour out His Spirit on His church, there were some of us who didn't like the way He was doing it. I mean, we could buy the "Praise the Lords" and even the upraised hands, but why on earth did all those gifts have to enter into it? Why couldn't the thing have been quieter and more polite!

And the "sides" and factions within the body realigned themselves in some cases, tightened up in other cases, and the stuff began to fly.

MEANWHILE, BACK IN A.D. 55 . . .

The church at Corinth had some problems similar to ours at the midway point in the first century. That is why I have selected I Corinthians 12 as the reference point for this book. When we think of Corinth, most of us think in terms of the tremendous moral problems present in that fellowship. Here were people getting stoned at the celebration of the Lord's table (I Corinthians 11). Brothers were even taking each other to court in civil suits.

But there was another problem in the church in that city that is sometimes overlooked, perhaps because it is not so dramatic and sensational, or maybe because it reflects an attitude too much like what we have within the people of God today. Because, you see, the body of Christ today possesses a major characteristic of Corinth: *we are split into factions* over God's work.

Read carefully what Paul said in his first letter to the Corinthians in about A.D. 55:

> Now I exhort you, brethren, by the name of our Lord Jesus Christ, that you all agree, and there be no divisions among you, but you be made complete in the same mind and in the same judgment.

> For I have been informed concerning you, my brethren, by Chloe's people, that there are quarrels among you.

> Now I mean this, that each of you is saying, "I am of Paul," and "I of Apollos," and "I of Cephas [Peter]," and "I of Christ."   (I Corinthians 1:10-12)

The believers in Corinth were in four camps: (1) those of Paul; (2) those of Apollos; (3) those of Peter; (4) those of Christ. They liked what particular men stood for and said, and began "groupies" to follow them. The three obvious sects were those who followed Paul, Apollos, and Peter; then there were the super-saints who said, "But we follow Christ!" Let's consider these four divisions briefly, for they reveal something about us moderns.

THE FOUR FACTIONS

The lines of demarcation for the first two groups are quite obvious. Paul was the man who planted the church at Corinth (I Corinthians 3:6). He was the one God used for eighteen months to get things started there. Apollos followed Paul's stay in that city (Acts 19:1) and was used by God to "water" or nourish the church. Apollos was a Grecian Jew who was a notable speaker and powerful in his handling of the Old Testament scriptures (Acts 18:24). It could be said that he was the "Bible teacher" who helped instruct these new believers.

Why believers in Corinth gathered themselves around Peter is not so clear. To our knowledge, Peter had never visited Corinth. But that the people had heard of him and knew of his service to the Lord is unmistakably clear from the manner in which Paul repeatedly makes reference to him (I Corinthians 1:12; 3:22; 9:5; 15:5). Could it be that he was known as the "head hauncho" among the apostles and thus venerated as "the man" by the church?

The group who said "We are of Christ" were those who discerned the fallacy of following after men, but who thought they were too good to associate with those who did. So they formed a fourth group, unified by their mutual distaste for factions, and instead of adopting a doctrinal statement they took on a messianic complex! (How subtle is the adversary.)

So here you have the four factions in Corinth as we might label them today:

1. THE TRADITIONALISTS ("Standing with historical foundation is the issue. We shall not be moved. Therefore, we will follow Brother Paul who came through the gates of Corinth first.")

2. THE BIBLE TRAINING ASSN. ("Bible knowledge is where it's at! Our man, Apollos, not only knows Scripture but he knows *Greek!*")

3. THE CHURCH RESTORATION MOVEMENT ("The church is the thing! If we ever expect to experience the continuation of the early church, we'd best stick with the man, Peter, on whom it was built!")

4. CORINTH FOR CHRIST, INC. ("You don't need Paul's foundation or Apollos's teaching or Peter's authority in the church. It's just walking with Jesus, man!")

21

You know what? Everyone had something of the truth. Is there for a moment anything wrong with a believer's wanting to take continuing counsel from the man who first influenced him for Christ? Or is it divisive to be under the teaching of a man mighty in the Scriptures? Is submitting oneself to the authority and wisdom of shepherds chosen by God to keep watch over the body of Christ a mistake? And who among us would knock just wanting to follow Christ? The reason for factionalism in Corinth was not that the men over whom the Corinthians were split were teaching error, though certainly false teaching has brought division at other times in history. One mark of sectarianism is that people follow men instead of God. And that was the very issue with which Paul confronted them.

The main reason for today's division over the gifts and ministries of the Holy Spirit is not primarily erroneous teaching, though certainly some is present. I am suggesting that the divisions in the body of Christ at this hour are essentially because people are following men instead of God. Today's schism is not even over the fact that some people possess certain spiritual gifts that other people do not possess. *The schism comes when the people who have certain gifts follow teachers who have essentially those same gifts, and when the people who do not possess those certain gifts follow teachers who do not have those gifts.*

Though division is present today just as it was in A.D. 55, the Corinthians had one thing going for them which we are missing today. Read I Corinthians 3:4-10; and see if you can notice what it is:

> For when one says, "I am of Paul," and another, "I am of Apollos," are you not mere men?

> What then is Apollos? And what is Paul? Servants through whom you believed, even as the Lord gave opportunity to each one.

> I planted, Apollos watered, but God was causing the growth.

22

So then neither the one who plants nor the one who waters is anything, but God who causes the growth.

Now he who plants and he who waters are one; but each will receive his own reward according to his own labor.

For we are God's fellow-workers; you are God's field, God's building.

According to the grace of God which was given to me, as a wise masterbuilder I laid a foundation, and another is building upon it. But let each man be careful how he builds upon it.

SCATTERED SHEPHERDS

The difference is, in the first century the workers were *united;* they were a team. Today, for the most part, the workers — Bible teachers, pastors, evangelists, etc. — are *divided.* Here was Paul, the victim of a vicious fourfold split in Corinth, telling the people that he and Peter and Apollos were *all* servants and fellow-workers of the Lord Jesus Christ (who unfortunately had become the titular head under human terms of the fourth group). Among the workers there was no division at all.

Now contrast that attitude with Christian leadership today! One man teaches, "Be careful not to associate with those who speak in tongues — they're divisive." Another will say, "Keep your fellowship only with fellow charismatics, and not with those who are ungifted, because they get you away from the gifts." A third will teach, "We know that though not every Christian has a *gift* of tongues, everyone can *speak* with tongues in his private prayer language." Still another, "Two kinds of tongues is ridiculous. Besides, those gifts passed away at the close of the apostolic era."

Whose side will you join? Or are there even more options for you to consider? It's a real dilemma, isn't it? But the point remains: the workers today are not together. And shepherds, not seeing the body of Christ, keep people following after them rather than God. Until our leadership comes together, the poor sheep are going to have a Heinz 57 variety of overseers from which to choose.

FIRST THINGS FIRST

Paul's first letter to Corinth answered a letter the Christians there had sent him. They had asked about sexual morality, meat sacrificed to idols and spiritual gifts (I Corinthians 7:1; 8:1; 12:1). In the last passage (12:1) Paul responded by saying he wanted no one to be ignorant about the gifts of the Spirit. But before he ever came to the question of spiritual gifts, or to any of the other questions, he first dealt with this matter of division in the body. To the apostle, division was a far more serious and basic problem than meat offered to idols, disagreements over the gifts, or even sexual immorality. These problems are symptomatic of not following Jesus Christ.

Today we could turn to the Scriptures and, as a body of believers, attempt to answer virtually every question there is concerning the gifts of the Spirit. Certainly the differences over these gifts, their uses, and even their existence are great within God's people. But far more basic than that problem is our attitude concerning the unity of the body.

Our current dilemma on manifestations of the Spirit is not the real problem, but a symptom of the real problem. We are not standing as one in Christ. Granted, answers are important, but not nearly so important as speaking with one voice about Jesus Christ, and stopping the division and strife. I truly believe (and I've seen it work) that if God's people will come together in love under the power of the Spirit and let Jesus rule as Head, ultimately the doctrinal truth will be manifest.

If we solve the whole "gifts dilemma" and do not have love for one another in Christ, it will profit us absolutely *nothing*. When we come, however, to a place of love among the brothers and the sisters in the Lord Jesus Christ, even the gifts problem won't be an issue. It will take care of itself!

three/ **Living by the Spirit**

> You know that when you were pagans, you were led
> astray to the dumb idols, however you were led. There-
> fore I make known to you, that no one speaking by the
> Spirit of God says "Jesus is accursed"; and no one can
> say, "Jesus is Lord," except by the Holy Spirit.
>
> (I Corinthians 12:2, 3)

Paul reminds the believers in Corinth that when they
were pagans — back before they believed in Jesus Christ —
they were led astray to "dumb idols." Idol worship was a
major pastime in Corinth, and chapter eight of First Corinthians deals with that issue.

In I Corinthians 12:3 Paul sets down a simple means of
knowing whether or not a person is speaking as a pagan or
speaking by the Holy Spirit as a regenerated believer. The

pagan will say Jesus is cursed, the one speaking by the Spirit will confess that Jesus is Lord.

THE BOMBAY BOMB

A brother who served Jesus Christ overseas for a number of years related an incident which first opened my eyes to the meaning of this verse. He was in a crowded train depot in Bombay, India. The place was teeming with people. This man was known to many people in that city for his walk with God.

While he was waiting for his train, a young man approached him and said, "Doesn't your Bible say that no man can say 'Jesus is Lord' except by the Holy Spirit?"

"That's right," said the missionary, sensing a trap and puzzled as to how this stranger knew he was a Christian.

"Well, Jesus is Lord," sneered the man defiantly.

The missionary related how he prayed for instant wisdom as to how to respond. He noticed a group of about eight or ten young Muslim men talking together nearby.

"Hey, men!" the Christian brother yelled awkwardly, trying to get their attention. "Here is one of your number talking to me who says *Jesus* is Lord!"

With a sudden motion, the "bold" young challenger, jolted with fear, spun around and darted out of the depot. In a flash he was gone. He had uttered the rhetoric that "Jesus is Lord," *but he could not say it and mean it.*

In our Western culture, where it is still relatively popular to be a Christian, it is far easier to fake it and say "Jesus is Lord" than it is in other parts of the world. But even the man with a false confession knows in his heart that his "faith" isn't real.

WILL THE REAL BELIEVER PLEASE STAND UP!

The scary thing is that a person can pretend he is a believer for such a length of time that even his own heart can become insulated to the truth and, in the end, deceive him. That is what Jesus is talking about in Matthew 7:21-23, when He says,

"Not every one who says to Me, 'Lord, Lord,' will enter the kingdom of heaven; but he who does the will of My Father, who is in heaven.

"Many will say to Me on that day, 'Lord, Lord, did we not prophesy in Your name, and in Your name cast out demons, and in Your name perform many miracles!'

"And then I will declare to them, 'I never knew you; depart from Me, you who practice lawlessness.' "

And talk about gifts and ministries! These people to whom Jesus is referring pulled off miracles, exorcism, and prophecies under the guise of Jesus' name, and *still* were fraudulent. Remember, Satan has a counterfeit for everything. *Everything.* Even the gifts and ministries of the Spirit can be made plastic.

Just because a person is into the supernatural has nothing at all to do with his walk with God. Jesus said, "By their fruits you shall know (recognize) them" (Matthew 7:20). Thus the *fruit* of the Spirit (love, joy, peace, patience, kindness, goodness, faithfulness, gentleness, self-control — Galatians 5:22, 23) take precedence even over the *gifts* of the Spirit. *Christian character is always before Christian ministry.*

How, then, can a man know if he is in relationship with Christ through the Holy Spirit? According to God's Word, one evidence is if he can say Jesus is Lord and really mean it. *My* mind says that's too simple. But that is, nonetheless, what God says.

THE GOOD, THE BAD, AND THE ODD

I have a close Christian friend who recently went through a real trial in his personal life. In the midst of his problem he became involved in something that had many earmarks of a cult.

The group didn't specialize in the "good news," though a measure of the Gospel was there. It wasn't actually into the "bad news" of denying Jesus Christ. It was more the "odd news" — something was wrong and you really couldn't put your finger on it. (And the "odd news" is often the most dangerous of all. When you have trouble pointing to a specific fault, but feel uneasy in a situation, be careful. The deceiver loves this atmosphere.)

After a while my friend left the "odd news" club and for a time was pretty much out-to-sea spiritually. Then he and another brother (who had gone about the same route) started getting together to search the Scriptures and to pray.

One day they decided some real repentance was needed on their part. They turned away from their attitudes of sectarianism and thinking of themselves more highly than was right, and they turned back to walking with the Lord.

"The thing that petrified me," my friend related, "was when I asked God to fill me with the Holy Spirit, nothing happened. I mean *nothing!*

"My first thought was that I had so hardened my heart to the Lord He had withdrawn His Spirit from me and would never fill me with the Spirit again. I really prayed in earnest and began crying out to God as I had never done before.

"One afternoon, as I was alone in the house, I was reading through First Corinthians chapter twelve. I came to verse three, and it hit me like a ton of bricks — 'no one can say, "Jesus is Lord," except by the Holy Spirit.'

"I put my Bible down on the floor next to my chair, looked up, and said, 'Jesus is Lord,' and I *knew* I had the Holy Spirit."

His statement of faith thrilled me! I knew he had the Holy Spirit, too. The witness was so evident. I understood I Corinthians 12:3 in a new way. If you can say "Jesus is Lord" with certainty, God says the Holy Spirit made you able to say it!

THE EYE OF FAITH

In the Word of God, the most often-quoted verse is Habakkuk 2:4, which appears over and over again in the New

Testament. Almost every Bible-reading Christian knows it by heart, though probably few of us have ever consciously memorized it: "The just shall live by faith." Faith is counting on the Lord to do it. Or, in some instances, it is believing that the Lord *has* done it or *will* do it. The *normal* attitude for a man of the Spirit is to believe God. If the Spirit of God is yours, then *expect* to walk by faith.

Faith does not depend upon my ability to believe; it is rather trusting in God's ability to deliver. God is faithful to carry out His promises. God is dependable to do *exactly* what He says He will do.

In a recent address in Dallas, Texas, the beloved Corrie Ten Boom, author of *The Hiding Place*, said that many times people come up to her and say, "Corrie, my, what great faith you have."

She smiled when she told how she replies back to them, "No, it's what a great God I have."

IT'S A TOGETHER TRINITY

Look at the fantastic promise Jesus gave to His followers in John 14:16-20:

> "And I will ask the Father, and He will give you another Helper, that He may be with you forever;

> that is the Spirit of truth, whom the world cannot receive, because it does not behold Him or know Him, but you know Him because He abides with you, and will be in you.

> "I will not leave you as orphans; I will come to you.

> "After a little while the world will behold Me no more, but you will behold Me; because I live, you shall live also.

> "In that day you shall know that I am in My Father, and you in Me, and I in you."

Now, consider the great truths set forth in that passage:
1. God will give you the Holy Spirit because Jesus asked Him to (v. 16).

2. The Holy Spirit will stay with you forever (v. 16)
3. The Holy Spirit of Truth will literally come to live *inside you* (v. 17).
4. The Holy Spirit will let God's people know (as on the day of Pentecost) that Jesus is in the Father, that we are in Jesus, and that Jesus is in us. Thus the Holy Spirit is God's divine hook-up with Jesus Christ (v. 20).

You see, God is ONE. You can't have one-third of God or two-thirds of God. You can only have all of God or none of God. If you have received Jesus Christ, you also have God the Father and God the Holy Spirit. This is true because Jesus promised the Holy Spirit would live within us who believe. Then, just a few verses later in John 14:23,

> Jesus answered and said to him, "If anyone loves Me, he will keep My word; and My Father will love him, and We will come to him, and make Our abode with him."

In that verse God the Father and God the Son *join* God the Holy Spirit in living inside you. And it all happens when you simply count on God to do it; when you fall in love with Him.

Now the question comes, "Is it possible to have God the Father, God the Son, and God the Holy Spirit inside you, and then blast off and live by your own power instead of by their power?" And that, really, is the problem with much of the body of Christ today. Because the answer is Yes. That's what "living by the flesh" means. This explains why Paul told the Galatians, "If we live by the Spirit, let us also walk by the Spirit" (Galatians 5:25).

And, you see, this is often where the misunderstanding comes in the matter of being filled with the Spirit.

ENERGY CRISIS

Here, for example, is a person who has been born of God, who has the Father, Son, and Holy Spirit living in him, but who is making it on human power and energy rather than on God's power and energy.

So this man comes under the teaching of a brother who is not only *born* of the Spirit, but *walking* by the Spirit. And the spiritual brother shares with the out-of-it brother that he can let the Holy Spirit *control* him, not just be in him.

So the carnal believer turns on and says, "Lord Jesus, control me with your Spirit. Fill me with your Holy Spirit." And Jesus does. But as is often the case, this newly turned-on brother rushes out and tells everyone that for the first time he's got the Holy Spirit. This is not really true. If he knew Jesus Christ, he *had* the Holy Spirit. The Holy Spirit just now got control of him. If you are a Christian, being filled with the Holy Spirit is not a matter of you getting more of the Holy Spirit; it's a matter of letting the Holy Spirit get more of you! At this point of surrender, you are in a new position to hear Him, obey Him, walk with Him.

THE CASE OF THE TWO TREES

Go back, for a minute, to the Garden of Eden. When Creation was complete, two trees were present in the garden: the tree of the knowledge of good and evil, and the tree of life. God told Adam and Eve to eat freely of the tree of life, but not to eat of the fruit of the tree of the knowledge of good and evil.

What were these two trees? The tree of the knowledge of good and evil was, simply, the tree that showed people the difference between what was right in the sight of God and what was wrong. Or, to put it into the context of the New Testament, the tree of the knowledge of good and evil was *the Law*. It was the Law, *before* it was even written down.

You see, the Law did not begin to exist when Moses received it on two tablets at Mount Sinai. The Law had existed from the start. It has been true from eternity past, and it will be true forever. The Law was true in the Garden of Eden when Cain killed Abel. To eat of that tree was tantamount to saying, "God, I can live in my own power just as long as I know what's right and wrong according to Your Law."

In contrast, there was the tree of life. This is the tree God meant for man to live by all along. The tree of life was God's life. It was the life given by the Father, the life by which the Son lived, and the life of the Holy Spirit. It was divine life. And it's the life that is ours when we receive Christ. It is the life you experience when the Holy Spirit comes upon you and causes you to walk in the light, and empowers you to do what He says.

In Adam's day, as in our day, there were two trees to live by, two methods of walking. One was by the rules, doing what God says is right and trying to avoid what is wrong. Or, there was the second way, and it is higher: to live by God's life from within you.

Now here's the thrilling part. When you live by God's life (i.e., when you walk in the Spirit) what does God promise will happen? Righteousness? Yes. Joy? Yes. Power? Yes. Gifts? Yes. Service? Yes. These, plus all else God supplies. Why? Because the life source is the same life source Jesus had. And everything that was His becomes ours, *because the source of life is the same.* It's *God's* life.

The man under flesh-control can't live by the Holy Spirit. The best the flesh can live by is the tree of the knowledge of good and evil — getting into what's right and wrong. Does that mean the rights aren't right and the wrongs aren't wrong? Heavens, NO! The rights are right and the wrongs are wrong. But there is a higher way to live than by rights and wrongs. And this is by the very life of God made real to us through the Holy Spirit. *The Holy Spirit is God's life!* When a man is Spirit-controlled, he can live by God's Spirit partaking of the tree of life.

THE THREEFOLD MAN

There are three parts to man — body, soul (or mind), and spirit (Figure 1).

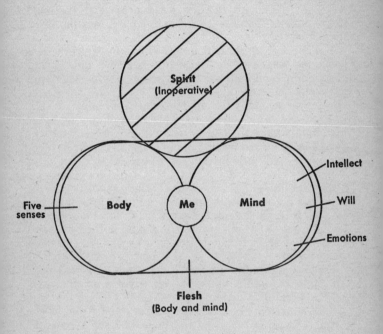

Figure 1. The Natural Man

The physical part of me navigates in the world via my five senses: touch, taste, smell, sight and sound.

The soul of a man is that part of him which thinks, wills to act, and has emotion. It's man's total personality, his being. The word "soul" in the New Testament is translated from the Greek word *psuche* from which we derive our word "psychology." Since we sometimes think "soul" is the same as "spirit" — and it's not — I will use the word "mind" instead.

The spirit of a man is that part of him by which he can know and perceive God. Since God is known through the Holy Spirit, and not known physically or mentally, the spirit must be made alive to Him. This is why Jesus said, "God is spirit; and those who worship Him must worship in spirit and truth" (John 4:24). Because of sin, my spirit by nature is dormant and inoperative. But when I turn to Jesus Christ, the Holy Spirit comes to live in me — He enters my spirit — and quite literally "turns me on" to God.

Before a person knows Jesus Christ, he operates only by his human life — his flesh — which is the combination of his body and his mind. In the physical realm he lives generally by what is pleasing to his senses. In his mind he is governed by his intellect (what he *thinks* he should do), by his emotions (what he *feels* like doing), and by his will (what he *wants* to do).

Of course, this arrangement gets us into some difficulty. The real "me," which resides in my body and mind, arrived on this scene damaged and bent. This is because the race of man to which I belong inherited sin through the fall of Adam. The Scripture says, "And those who are in the flesh cannot please God" (Romans 8:8). If my identity is only with the flesh, I am incapable of knowing God and of being a part of His will and kingdom.

On the cross Jesus Christ paid for all my sin, both original and experiential, and tore down all the barriers that kept me from God. But even before He died, He promised the Holy Spirit would come and live in the lives of all who trust Him.

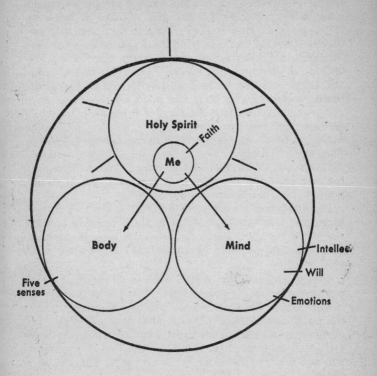

Figure 2. The Spiritual Man

35

When I turn from living by my life to living by Christ, the Holy Spirit takes up residence inside me and makes me alive to God (Figure 2). Romans 8:9 says of believers, "However you are not in the flesh but in the Spirit, if indeed the Spirit of God dwells in you. But if anyone does not have the Spirit of Christ, he does not belong to Him."

God's desire is not *just* for the Holy Spirit to live inside me; He wants me to be controlled by the Spirit. And as the Spirit controls *me,* my body and mind are His. I still have my five senses, but *He* is my *life.* I still have intellect, will, and emotion, but they are influenced by the Holy Spirit instead of by my human life. The real me becomes elevated; *I live in the Spirit.*

Growing in Christ, then, is a matter of logging time under the control of the Holy Spirit. It is counting on the Holy Spirit to lead me moment by moment.

It is important I see myself in Christ as a *total person* — body, soul, and spirit — and not as three separate entities. For when my spirit becomes alive to His Spirit, new life also comes to my body (Romans 8:11) and to my mind (Romans 8:6).

Sometimes — and this is true even in Christian circles — people are taught the newness of their spirits at the expense of (or even to the virtual denial of) how God sees and refreshes their redeemed physical and personal selves. Remember as you walk in the Spirit that God holds your body and mind in great dignity and worth. The new physical you and mental you belong to Him to serve Him, to learn of Him.

WELCOME BACH

Say that you are into music, and you feel the greatest composer who ever lived was Johann Sebastian Bach. You decide that you would like to compose music of the same quality as Bach.

So you travel abroad, study in the great conservatories of Europe, visit historic cathedrals and libraries where this man has had an influence, and set out to emulate his composition.

Then it happens. You fail! You just can't do it. You come to the conclusion that the only way possible for a man to ever reach the heights of Bach would be if, in some mysterious way, J. S. Bach could come back to life in nonmaterial form and live inside your body. Then, perhaps, you could compose music like Bach's.

We sometimes do the same thing with Jesus Christ! We look at His life and say, "I want to be like that. Since He was God, and He lived the right way, I should seek to emulate Him." And how far do we get?

It's like the old New Year's Eve scene when everyone makes resolutions. They last for a week or so. Or I go to summer camp and decide to turn over a new leaf. But two or three days after I come home I'm worse than I was before.

But if there were some way I could get Jesus Christ back from the dead and live in — wait a minute! That's happened! That's what the resurrection and the Holy Spirit are all about. God has already done it in history.

Today, if you have never done so, place your trust in Jesus Christ. He will enter your life the instant you begin to count on Him and will begin to live through you. If you have already placed your faith in Jesus Christ, but have never really counted on Him to immerse you in His Holy Spirit, count on Him to do it right now. Take of His life. Walk in His Spirit.

As you open your heart, receive from Him all that He has and all that He is. The gifts He has for you are *yours*. The role of service — the part you play in His body: the believers everywhere, the local assembly of those called by Him — which He has for you is now *yours*. It will develop, it will mature, it will grow. But claim it, for it belongs to you.

For He is our *life*.

four/ Life, Not Lingo

> Now there are varieties of gifts, but the same Spirit. And there are varieties of ministries, and the same Lord. And there are varieties of effects, but the same God who works all things in all persons. But to each one is given the manifestation of the Spirit for the common good. (1 Corinthians 12:4-7)

The first characteristic of God revealed to man was through the pen of Moses in Genesis 1:1: "In the beginning God created. . . ." He was unveiled first as a *creator*, and He does not change. He was creative then and He is creative now.

A Variety of Manifestations

There is one common word to each of the three verses quoted above, the word "varieties." A creative God produces variety. You and I will serve Him differently, have different spiritual abilities, and produce different results. He *promises* variety on the front end.

The way into God's domain is narrow; it is the way of the Cross. The broad way, man's way, leads to destruction. The narrow way, God's way through Jesus Christ and Him alone, leads to life. Once inside that domain, the Holy Spirit produces variety. There is a variety of gifts, ministries, and results that appear in people's lives once they enter through that narrow door.

ONENESS OF SPIRIT

But God does not say there are a variety of Holy Spirits — and this is important to see! There is not a Baptist Holy Spirit, a Pentecostal Holy Spirit, a Lutheran Holy Spirit, a Full Gospel Businessmen's Fellowship International Holy Spirit or Church of Christ Holy Spirit or the Covenant vs. Dispensational theology Holy Spirit. There is one Holy Spirit, and that is God's Holy Spirit. Within God's Holy Spirit, there is fantastic variety and creativeness. He passes out a variety of gifts, a variety of ministries, and produces a variety of results.

Let me run another list by you, except in this list I'm going to mention names of men I greatly admire as believers in Jesus and greatly respect. There is not a Watchman Nee Holy Spirit, a Demos Shakarian Holy Spirit, a Billy Graham Holy Spirit, a John Wesley Holy Spirit, a Keith Miller Holy Spirit, an Oral Roberts Holy Spirit, an Alexander Campbell Holy Spirit, an Apostle Paul Holy Spirit, a You Holy Spirit or a Me Holy Spirit. There is only God's Holy Spirit.

In just reading these brothers' names, we are reminded that God's Holy Spirit has done a great variety of things through them. Their gifts? Different. Their ministries? Different. The results produced? Different. But they have lived by the same Holy Spirit.

GIFTS

What are spiritual gifts? The word "gift" is taken from

39

the Greek word *charisma*, which means a favor granted without any merit. A gift is an instrument or a tool God gives to His son or daughter to carry out a certain task. A tool — not a weapon, mind you — but a tool! Gifts are never given to tear up the body of Christ, but always to make it more of a functioning unit.

MINISTRIES

The ministries of the Spirit are the varied ways in which the Holy Spirit relates to us. To minister means to serve. God's Spirit ministers to us through: the baptism of the Spirit, the filling of the Spirit, the leading of the Spirit, the sealing of the Spirit, the anointing of the Spirit, and the earnest of the Spirit.

There are also a variety of ways in which we minister to or serve one another. One man's ministry may be very different from the next man's, while both are led by God. In fact, there are other ministries around with which we simply do not agree.

When I was young, our family would take periodic vacations up on the "North Shore" of Lake Superior. I can remember as we passed through Duluth, Minnesota, and on up toward Lutsen, there would be signs painted on rocks along the shoreline drive which said "Jesus Saves" and "Repent or Perish."

Those signs bugged me no end. Part of it may have been the rebellion of my aesthetic nature, seeing that bright, glossy paint dripping down and hardened in the crevasses of the rocks. At any rate, open-air signs never did seem to me to be appropriate.

But I've ceased being critical of "Jesus Saves" signs. A few years ago I met a man who gave his life to Christ through one of those (as I thought then) obnoxious signs. And the Lord has used him in many powerful ways. Even though signs aren't my bag, I can no longer knock them.

The same is true with "hell, fire, and damnation" radio preachers. They really gross me out. And it's not because I disagree with them — there really *is* a hell, and there'll be fire and damnation for the wicked. No problem there. But why does the gravel-throated message have to be the same five days a week . . . *plus* the offering!

But, you know, there are people who come to Christ through these broadcasts. I'm convinced there are some folks who need to be dangled over the pit to get them to listen. I'd never have come that way. I'd heard about hell. What I was interested in was a God who cared for me enough to send His Son to die for me so I could be made a new person. And I find my ministry today is geared far more along those lines: a positive proclamation of Jesus Christ.

When somebody I'm visiting with willfully rejects Christ, however, guess what my message is? I tell him of the alternative to God's love. Wrath. And flames. For all time. But the alternative is not the core of my message. Christ is.

God says there are varieties of ministries. That's His plan and I accept it completely. And knowing of His variety certainly makes those we disagree with into beautiful believers with whom we can know oneness.

EFFECTS

There is a great difference in the effects or results or the outworkings of the Holy Spirit. Sometimes His work produces quiet awe, sometimes noisy shouts of "Right On!" and "Praise the Lord!" There are times when the Spirit of God works earnest repentance in people's hearts; other times people laugh with joy in His presence. Sometimes His work produces surprise, at other times the fulfillment of something everyone knew would happen. In one instance He works fast, in another slowly. Sometimes His response is affirmative, at other times negative.

MANIFESTATIONS OF THE SPIRIT — WHY?

After Paul introduces the three manifestations of the Holy Spirit — the gifts, the ministries, and the effects — he sets down a principle which much of Christendom has forgotten

41

today. The main purpose of the work of the Holy Spirit today is for the mutual building up of the body of Christ, and not for a personal spiritual "zap" for those through whom the Spirit works. Though there is something very personally rewarding for the believer who is exercising his gift or partaking in a ministry, the work of the Holy Spirit is for the common good of God's people. "But to each one is given the manifestation of the Spirit for the common good" (I Corinthians 12:7).

I, frankly, feel very, very fulfilled when I am engaged in the work of evangelism. That's my number-one calling, and I am happier when I am helping to reach people for the kingdom of God than at almost any other time. I know of brothers who have the gift of teaching, and they say the most satisfying element of their Christian lives is when they are setting forth the Word of God to their fellows in the body of Christ. Those of our number who exercise the manifestation of tongues feel deeply moved and drawn close to the throne of God as they express their secret concerns to God via this unknown language. Those utilizing the gift of helps will quickly tell you that it *is* more blessed to give than to receive, and that helping others — especially those of the household of faith — brings its own reward.

But as real as these impressions are, the ultimate purpose of the work of God's Spirit is not so much for the personal satisfaction of the person through whom He is working — though that is there — as it is for the upbuilding of the body of Christ. In this existential age, so much of the emphasis is upon "what turns me on." But what about that which turns the whole body of Christ on, or even what turns God on? That's part of the program too!

RHETORIC OR REALITY?

So often we get romanced by the *words* we use rather than by what is being *communicated* through these words. A real red-flag word today is the "baptism" of the Holy Spirit. It really hurts to use that word in some circles and get boooooooooed, and to use it in other circles and receive spontaneous applause. Certainly "baptized with the Spirit" is a valid phrase contained within the pages of holy Writ. But let's get excited over its meaning, rather than because of its usage at the proper time and in the proper place.

THE PREDICTION JESUS MADE

In Acts 1:5 Jesus promises His disciples that they "shall be baptized with the Holy Spirit not many days from now." The English word "baptize" is transliterated from the Greek word *baptizo*, which means to immerse, to plunge into, or to be identified with. There is no English equivalent of this word, so the translators coined the word "baptize" to bring the concept over into the English language.

Virtually all biblical scholars will agree that the baptism with the Holy Spirit to which Jesus referred here came at Pentecost.

But here's an interesting phenomenon. On the day of Pentecost, as recorded in Acts 2, the event that Jesus prophesied took place, yet the word "baptized," in describing the Holy Spirit's work that day, is not used! Instead the Word of God records the event in this manner:

And when the day of Pentecost had come, they were all together in one place.

And suddenly there came from heaven a noise like a violent, rushing wind, and it filled the whole house where they were sitting.

And there appeared to them tongues as of fire distributing themselves, and they rested on each one of them.

And they were all filled with the Holy Spirit and began to speak with other tongues, as the Spirit was giving them utterance.   (Acts 2:1-4)

The word used to describe what Jesus said would happen is "filled," an absolutely different word in the Greek. Does that mean someone copped out on the usage of the word *baptizo*? Not at all. What it does mean is that God is bigger than *words*. He is not, and cannot be, confined to a single term in man's language. God moves in the area of truth and reality, and words only *describe* what He is doing. Is this, then, a point for the one who would prefer not to talk about the baptism of the Holy Spirit? Not at all. It simply means God is beyond confinement to the term, "baptized with the Holy Spirit."

At the end of Acts 2 when Peter was finishing his message, the listeners were moved to respond to what he was saying. They said, "'Brethren, what shall we do?' And Peter said to them, 'Repent, and let each of you be baptized in the name of Jesus Christ for the forgiveness of your sins; and you shall receive the gift of the Holy Spirit. For the promise is for you and your children, and for all who are far off'" (Acts 2:37-39).

When Peter finished speaking, a whole lot of people were baptized with the Holy Spirit. There was no mention of speaking with unknown tongues, but we know it was the baptism of the Spirit, because the word "promise" was used, and Jesus promised the baptism of the Spirit. Do you see what *word* is missing? It's the word "baptized" — it's just not used here. Instead, Peter's phraseology of "you shall *receive the gift of the Holy Spirit*" was used. Why? Why wasn't the term "baptized with the Spirit" used? I don't know — unless, of course, we have a God who is not hung up on terms. And we do! God is not partial to *terms*, He's partial to *truth*. It's not *rhetoric*, it's *reality*. God is all for submerging people with the Holy Spirit, but He does so with *life*, not with *lingo*.

Let's go a bit further through the book of Acts, and chase down the results of that same initial promise the Lord Jesus Christ made concerning the baptism of the Holy Spirit. Because, you will find that still more variation comes in the words which describe the fulfillment of His initial promise. Consider Acts 8:14-17:

Now when the apostles in Jerusalem heard that Samaria

44

had received the word of God, they sent them Peter and John.

who came down and prayed for them, that they might receive the Holy Spirit.

For He had not yet fallen upon any of them; they had simply been baptized in the name of the Lord Jesus.

Then they began laying their hands on them, and they were receiving the Holy Spirit.

In this passage two verbs — "fallen upon" and "receiving" — are used to describe the work of the Holy Spirit. Bear in mind that these are people to whom the Holy Spirit has never been ministered before, and yet now they are receiving Him. This is also a direct fulfillment of the earlier promise of the Lord Jesus in Acts 1. Here the truth of the baptism of the Spirit is being set forth, but in different words.

In Acts 10, the work of the Holy Spirit extends through the Apostle Peter out to the Gentiles. The man standing as exhibit A in this case is Cornelius, a military commandant in the Italian regiment. Peter, prompted by a vision from God, comes and presents the gospel of Christ to this man and his household. While Peter is yet speaking, the Holy Ghost falls upon the group and draws the family to a relationship with the Lord Jesus. It's part of the fulfillment of Jesus' promise in Acts 1, but the terminology is still missing. Because here the two verbs "fall upon" and "poured out" are used in describing the Spirit's work:

While Peter was still speaking these words, the Holy Spirit fell upon all those who were listening to the message.

And all the circumcised believers who had come with Peter were amazed, because the gift of the Holy Spirit had been poured out upon the Gentiles also.

For they were hearing them speaking with tongues and exalting God. Then Peter answered,

"Surely no one can refuse the water for these to be

baptized who have received the Holy Spirit just as we
did, can he?" (Acts 10:44-47)

The last instance in the Book of Acts where the Holy
Spirit comes upon the uninitiated is in chapter nineteen.
Here we are dealing with a group of Old Testament believers, disciples of John the Baptist. These men knew well
the promises of God, but did not know the Son of God who
fulfilled these promises. Thus when Paul asked them if they
had received the Holy Spirit since they believed, they were
flabbergasted. "We haven't even heard of the Holy Spirit,"
they responded.

With some further questioning it was discovered these
men knew that Jesus Christ was on His way, but did not
know that He had already come. Here is what happened:

And it came about that while Apollos was at Corinth,
Paul having passed through the upper country came
to Ephesus, and found some disciples, and he said to
them, "Did you receive the Holy Spirit when you believed?" And they said to him, "No, we have not even
heard whether there is a Holy Spirit."

And he said, "Into what then were you baptized?" And
they said, "Into John's baptism."

And Paul said, "John baptized with the baptism of
repentance, telling the people to believe in Him who
was coming after him, that is, in Jesus."

And when they heard this, they were baptized in the
name of the Lord Jesus.

And when Paul had laid his hands upon them, the
Holy Spirit came on them, and they began speaking
with tongues and prophesying. (Acts 19:1-6)

The gist of the conversation uncovered the fact that it
isn't enough to repent, but that you must receive new life
in Christ. So they did. And when Paul laid his hands upon
them to receive the Holy Spirit, the verb used is that the
Spirit "came on" them, and then they began speaking with

tongues and prophesying. This has to be the same promise Jesus Christ made in Acts 1, yet the word "baptize" still is not used. Does that mean they were not baptized with the Spirit? No! The Spirit came on them, and they spoke with tongues. The life was there, but the word "baptized" was not.

These examples make me wonder if, while looking to the tree of life for reality, for life, we are not at the same time looking to the tree of the knowledge of good and evil for the "correct" words and sounds to describe what is going on.

five/ The Gifts: Knowing, Trusting, Healing

For to one is given the word of wisdom through the
Spirit, to another the word of knowledge according to
the same Spirit; to another faith by the same Spirit,
and to another gifts of healing by the one Spirit.

(I Corinthians 12:8, 9)

In these next three chapters I want to consider some of
the various gifts of the Holy Spirit. Earlier we talked about
spiritual gifts as being tools or instruments given to the
body of Christ to be used in the accomplishment of tasks
at hand.

Some of my early Christian training taught me to *smor-
gasbord* the gifts, using only those which were said to be

applicable for today and leaving behind the ones which were for another time in history. But the almost wholesale re-entry of the gifts in the church has caused me to take a second look. I've had to eat some theological crow along the way! A review of these spiritual instruments is in order — especially now when they have become such a focal point of attention in the family of God.

In I Corinthians 12:8 Paul begins to name off some of the various gifts of the Spirit. Though this particular list is not exhaustive, it is a good cross-section of gifts for us to consider. I will spend more time on some of these than on others, hoping to reveal the essence of these gifts and how they function.

THE WORD OF WISDOM

Do you ever wonder, after talking with another believer, how that person could have such fantastic insight into the things of God — insights that you seemingly have not had? You marvel at his or her ability to assess a situation in the light of spiritual truth and come up with an uncanny analysis. The Scriptures call it the "word of wisdom."

I have on occasion experienced the gift, but most often when I need wisdom I seek out others who possess this gift. As far as its personal use goes, special wisdom from the Spirit for me comes most often when I am in a counseling situation and need the mind of the Lord on a matter.

Have you ever found yourself conversing with another person and all of a sudden been awestruck at the astonishing truths coming from your lips? Advice and exhortation come through you which you know on the basis of God's Word are true, yet which you never consciously learned? Most likely, it was the Lord giving to you a word of wisdom.

Jesus promised the word of wisdom to believers in Matthew 10:19, 20, as He forewarned His disciples of impending cross-examination of their faith by the world:

"But when they deliver you up, do not become anxious

49

about how or what you will speak; for it shall be given you in that hour what you are to speak.

"For it is not you who speak, but it is the Spirit of your Father who speaks in you."

Lay claim to that promise, for the Spirit of God is more than willing to speak through you if you are simply open and available to Him.

In the Book of Acts there are several instances in which believers spoke with wisdom beyond themselves. Peter, with John at his side, laid a heavy message on members of a big-time religious council, in Acts 4:8-12. The account of the message begins by saying that Peter was "filled with the Holy Spirit" as he spoke (v. 8). And look at the response of the councilmen when he finished (v. 13): "Now as they [the council] observed the confidence of Peter and John, and understood that they were uneducated and untrained men, they were marveling, and began to recognize them as having been with Jesus."

THE WORD OF KNOWLEDGE

Whereas the word of *wisdom* is the application of God's truth to circumstances and situations, by a word of *knowledge,* the Spirit reveals to you specific facts and data which you could never know apart from the Spirit. The word of knowledge is similar to a prophetic utterance, but is distinguished by the fact that it deals with the present instead of the future.

Jesus was given a word of knowledge when He instructed His disciples in Matthew 21:2 to go to an adjacent village and bring back a donkey and her colt that would be awaiting them. Jesus had no prior information that the animals were there: the Holy Spirit gave Him His information.

Peter employed the gift of knowledge in Acts 5:1-3:

But a certain man named Ananias, with his wife Sapphira, sold a piece of property,

and kept back some of the price for himself, with his

wife's full knowledge, and bringing a portion of it, he laid it at the apostles' feet.

But Peter said, "Ananias, why has Satan filled your heart to lie to the Holy Spirit, and to keep back some of the price of the land?"

Without the aid of a pocket calculator or a blue book of land prices, the apostle, through knowledge given him by the Holy Spirit, put his finger on the dishonest report.

When we lived in Memphis, Tennessee, and I was on the administrative staff of Memphis State University, we had a Sunday night open house each week. The crowd usually numbered sixty to eighty, and we would sing together, share what the Lord had been doing in our lives during the week, lift up the Lord in prayer, study the Word of God, intercede for any who were sick, and do whatever else the Lord had on His docket.

One evening, just after the singing began, a girl who was a new sister in the Lord walked in, and with her was the president of one of the MSU fraternities. It surprised me that he was there. The singing and sharing were unusually alive that night, and everyone left with lifted spirits.

After the meeting was over, I walked up and introduced myself to Don and thanked him for coming. "I've never heard singing like this in my life!" he said, looking around at the kids who remained. "And there was no songleader to keep them going, either. They really sang because they wanted to — and they meant it."

Then the tone of his voice became more serious. "Do you suppose we could talk alone for a minute?" he asked.

We walked out toward the kitchen and pulled up two chairs around our large, round oak table in the breakfast room. I cannot remember exactly how the conversation began, but Don was voicing his need to know Jesus Christ. He told how he had been to some of the outstanding Christian conference programs in different parts of the country and had really heard about Christ, but had never given his life over to the Lord.

51

At one point in the discussion, *I* began to tell *him* some details about his past. I told him some of his problems, some of his sins. I brought out things that nobody knew except Don and the Lord.

"Who told you this?" he asked.

"No one," I answered. "All I can tell you is that God is giving me this information right now."

"Wow!" he responded abruptly. "Let's pray."

And at that moment, he gave his life to Christ.

All the while this was going on, it never occurred to me that I was experiencing the spiritual gift of knowledge. It wasn't until a few days later as I was reading the Bible that God revealed to me just what had happened.

And as I got to know Don I began to see *why* it had happened. He had heard the Gospel over and over and over again since he was small, and he had systematically turned down Jesus Christ at every hand. He needed something supernatural to convince him of the truth. God graciously supplied that need through the word of knowledge.

You know, when a spiritual gift happens, there's nothing weird or spooky connected with it, because God isn't weird or spooky. In fact, if those characteristics are present, the experience is bogus. When God does something, it is very solid and real. It's supernatural, to be sure, but not eerie.

While the Lord was speaking His word of knowledge through me, my voice didn't get any higher, nor my eyes stare and bulge. In fact, other than being aware that I was dispersing information I had never learned, I was totally unaware by feelings that anything out of the ordinary was going on. It *felt* no different than walking in the Spirit ever does!

I bring this out, because a lot of people are spooked over spiritual gifts. And there's no need to be. When God purposes to perform a miracle, and you are walking in the Spirit, that miracle is absolutely the most normal event that could occur at that moment. You *know* it's just what the Lord ordered.

It may be Satan has pulled off a counterfeit spiritual gift which you've witnessed, and for this reason "the gifts" bug you. Or maybe someone has exercised his gift in the flesh, and for that reason you're leery. Or perhaps a brother who has been prejudiced against the gifts has warned you to reject the very mention of spiritual gifts, so you've been educated against them.

I'm not trying to say, "Rush out, and jump into the first thing that comes along resembling a spiritual gift." What I am saying is, as you live by the life of the Holy Spirit within you, and you walk in the truth of His Word, you can expect under normal conditions for the gifts of the Spirit to operate when they're needed. Don't be afraid of them. For sure, God is not out to startle you! But He does want to be about the building and repairing of the body of Christ, and one of the ways He has chosen to accomplish this task is through the use of tools — the gifts of the Spirit.

THE GIFT OF FAITH

As we have already discussed, walking by faith is the means by which God has planned for *all* to live in Christ. In addition to faith for the daily walk with God, there is a special *gift of faith*. This gift is given to handle the "tough" situations above and beyond the normal call of duty.

The question may come, "Well, how do I know when I need the gift of faith, or should I just live by 'regular' faith?" You don't know, and better still, you don't need to know. All God asks is that you walk trusting Him, and He'll provide everything else you need — including the gift of special faith.

One of my most memorable experiences of receiving an extra measure of faith came when God gave us the go-ahead to buy our first house when we lived in Evanston, Illinois. I could literally write a whole book on how it all came about, and maybe someday I will. But there was one isolated incident that to me was fantastic.

We had just come from our bank, where I had drawn

53

out all but a few dollars from my account to make the down-payment, and were driving over to the bank where the closing was to take place. Marilyn and I were alone in the car and very much aware we were out of money. I mean, not low but out! And to make matters even more interesting, I was unemployed. But we knew God had led us to buy the place.

And halfway from the first bank to the second — they were about a mile apart — I prayed out loud and said, "Lord, *somehow* would you please supply us with $100 today." And I knew as soon as those words came forth that the Lord had put that prayer on my heart, and it was as good as answered.

We sat through all the legal entanglements of the closing, signed all the proper papers, exchanged necessary checks, shook hands with the banker, the lawyers, the former owner and his wife, and headed out of the bank to the parking lot. We were thrilled beyond words to own our very first house, but were well aware of our financial privation. We got into the car and closed the doors; I started the engine and headed for the exit.

As I was reaching into my pocket for the small customer parking token supplied at the bank to unlock the exit gate, I noticed the former owner of the house running toward us with a big smile. He had an envelope in his hand. I slowed down and lowered the window.

"I really feel bad that I was unable to clean all the trash out of the upstairs back room," he said. "This will help pay the junk man to haul it all away."

"Thanks, Bob," I said, opening the envelope to take out what I assumed could not have been more than ten or fifteen dollars. I almost cried when I saw the check for one hundred bucks.

"There's no way I can take this," I told him, thinking back to how we had already talked him down to below what the place was worth.

"No, my wife and I just discussed it, and we want you to have it," he said firmly. I knew he meant it.

"You won't believe this, Bob, but you're answered prayer!" I told him how we had prayed, and thanked him profusely.

And it was miracle after miracle like this which convinced us — even in the face of horrible financial odds — that God wanted us to have that house. And the Lord reinforced His will for us through a gift, the gift of faith.

Sometimes the statement is made that spiritual gifts do not operate apart from the gathered body of Christ. Spiritual gifts do not happen *apart from* the body of Christ, but the body of Christ functions whether it is *gathered or not.* Because as individual members of the body walk in the Spirit, the body functions. Even when one member experiences a gift of the Spirit, that gift is still given for the common good.

As we walk by faith in the power of the Holy Spirit, we can expect the supernatural to happen all the time, not just when the brothers and sisters come together in the Lord.

GIFTS OF HEALING

One of the most "sensational" gifts of the Spirit is the gift of healing. In fact, next to the gift of tongues, I suppose more people get uptight over the matter of spiritual healing than with just about any other issue.

My first encounter with "faith healing" was a gruesome episode. I had been a Christian about a year. Marilyn and I were on our way to Dallas from Minneapolis and were driving through Kansas City. On the left-hand side of the road I spotted a huge tent and a sign saying, "Miracle Revival."

"It's one of those old-fashioned Southern revivals that we've heard about," I told her. "Let's grab dinner and go back to see what's going on." We found a motel, unpacked, ate, and got back to the tent about 7:30.

I knew the moment I walked inside the tent something was wrong. At many gatherings of the saints where I'd been, there was present a sweet, fragrant spirit. Such an atmosphere was noticeably absent on this occasion. Just ahead of us two ladies were prostrate, rolling in the dust of the aisle.

Up front an outfit louder than "Chicago" was throbbing out the most hideous religious music I have ever heard. The guy leading the sideshow was waving a pair of crutches in his hand, purportedly taken from someone who had just been "healed," while the rest of his body was doing the bump and grind, keeping time to the music. People were yelling out, "Jesus! Jesus!" You could hear long, strung out "Halleluuuuuuuuuujahs" all over the place, and the Spirit of God within me said, "This is not of Me."

"Let's get out of here," I said to Marilyn. We made for the exit. A woman grabbed my arm just as we went through the tent door and said, "Would you give me a ride?" She had a strange, almost deathly look in her eyes.

The Lord said "No" to me, and I said "Sorry" to her, and we split for the car.

Several years later, while reading the newspaper one morning, I came across the name of the man who led the "revival," in a small headline on one of the inside pages. He had died. The article said he succumbed to acute alcoholism. When the story hit the wire services, his board released the following statement: "The important thing is not so much his life, as the message he preached."

I couldn't believe it.

Man, if the message was no better than to produce that result, it wasn't worth anything in the first place. The whole thing, as far as I was concerned, was straight from the pit.

That incident had an unfortunate, on-going result for me, because Satan used that event for years to keep me from believing God heals today. Even to the extent that one evening when a couple who had known Christ for two weeks called and told us that the night before their daughter had run a 104° fever, and they prayed "just like in the

Bible" and asked Jesus to heal her — and *He* did — I cautioned them not to get started on "that sort of thing."

Do you know what changed my mind? God. God did. And it was through people who I knew walked in the Spirit who were healed physically.

A critic of healing could say at this point, "Well, you're just building your theology on your experience. You should base your views of healing on what the Bible says about it." That's exactly right. But you see, what I had done was to take all those verses in the Bible which talked about healing and explain them away. Therefore the only thing the Lord had left through which to teach me was the miracle itself. And when I saw normal, loving, Spirit-filled believers experience healing, what more could I say but "God, I guess my theology has been wrong!"

I was in the locker room at a Memphis gym with a good friend one afternoon, getting ready to play handball. "I've got something really great to tell you," my friend said.

"Friday night, a bunch of us got together for ice cream and cake at a friend's house. It was after an evangelistic meeting, and I suppose there were about fifty of us there.

"A gal walked in with a large bandage over her eye. We asked her what had happened. She said she was a dental technician and she was grinding down some bridgework the day before and a particle had flown into her right eye. They rushed her to the doctor, and he told her she had gone blind in that eye and could lose the sight of her other eye.

"I asked her why she thought it had happened. She said, 'I guess the Lord wanted to make me more humble.' That just didn't sit right with me. So I told her, 'If it takes going blind to make us more humble, I think we all should pray we go blind. I believe the Lord let this happen to you to glorify Himself.' And she agreed.

"Then I said, 'How many of you people here believe if we were to lay hands on this sister right now and pray that

57

she be healed — how many of you will join me right now and pray for her?'

"Five ladies stepped up. We had the girl sit down in a chair, and then these five sisters and I laid hands on her and claimed that she be healed in Jesus' name. When we finished praying, she took off the bandages, somebody handed her a dictionary to read, and she could see perfectly!"

I was so thrilled, I didn't know what to say. That was beautiful! This brother didn't run with the "healing crowd," either. These were just a group of conservative, nice, suburban Christians.

He went on to say she went back to the doctor the next day and it absolutely startled him. The doctor couldn't believe it.

It was Friday night when she was healed, she saw the doctor Saturday, and we were playing handball on Monday — three days later. During the course of the game, my friend took a wild slice at the ball and jammed his middle finger against the side wall. He yelped with pain.

Now here, to me, is the interesting thing. We had just been talking about this great miracle. Someone was healed of blindness. Now, three days later, the same guy who believes God for a healing Friday night has just jammed his finger. It is beginning to swell to twice its size.

I say to him, "This may sound funny to you, but I have absolutely no compulsion at all to pray that your finger be healed."

"I don't either," he says. So he runs back up to the locker room, gets it taped, and we go on playing.

The lesson in this is spectacular for me. The issue in healing is not healing in itself. It is walking in the Spirit. The flesh *loves* to build on events and to put God under pressure to do it again, the same way. But the Spirit is creative. The flesh, when one healing happens, is tempted to run off and form a big international movement to promote healings. The Spirit says, "No, it's My job to heal. You just walk in My life. Don't live by My miracles. Live by Me. You see, I do it differently each time. I'm a God of variety."

Brothers and sisters, we are told to "walk in the Spirit" (Galatians 5:16). Not "fly in the Spirit," "run in the Spirit," "limp in the Spirit," "dive in the Spirit," but "walk in the Spirit." And walking takes more faith than any of the others. Because with the others, we set our *own* pace. But God's pace is a walk.

six / The Gifts: Prophecy and Discernment

And to another the effecting of miracles, and to another prophecy, and to another the distinguishing of spirits.
(I Corinthians 12:10a)

THE EFFECTING OF MIRACLES

The "miracles" mentioned in the passage above are not so much a *gift* as they are an *effect* from a gift. That is why the phrase reads, "the effecting [literally, 'the effects'] of miracles." Miracles are not gifts in and of themselves, but rather the result of the gifts in operation.

THE GIFT OF PROPHECY

For years it was felt in many Christian circles that the gift of prophecy in this age was the ability to take the prophetic portions of the Scripture and expound upon them. "Prophecy Conferences" would gather to consider truths surrounding the imminent return of Jesus Christ to the earth. Men with "prophetic gifts" would be the Bible teachers at these conferences.

But with the great resurgence of direct "thus says the Lord" prophecy in the body of Christ at this hour, many students of the Scripture are taking a second look at this gift.

In the Scriptures the utterance of prophecy can be broken down into two categories: (1) that which becomes the recorded, written word; and (2) that which remains only a spoken word as instruction just for the moment. Here is a sampling of each category:

WRITTEN	ORAL
The prophecy of Isaiah is being fulfilled, which says... (Matthew 13:14)	Judas and Silas, also being prophets themselves, . . . strengthened the brethren with a lengthy message. (Acts 15:32)
No prophecy of Scripture is a matter of one's own interpretation. (II Peter 1:20)	
Do not seal up the words of the prophecy of this book. (Revelation 22:10)	Now this man had four virgin daughters who were prophetesses. (Acts 21:9)
This is what was spoken of through the prophet Joel. (Acts 2:16)	But one who prophesies speaks to men for edification and exhortation and consolation. (I Corinthians 14:3)
	At this time some prophets came down from Jerusalem to Antioch. (Acts 11:27)

Just as with the other gifts, in prophecy there are the genuine and the counterfeit. The Lord Jesus Christ warned His disciples of false prophets (Matthew 7:15; 24:11, 24), and later when some of these same men authored the New Testament epistles, the warning was repeated (II Peter 2:1; I John 4:1).

In the Old Testament the people wanted to know whether or not they could believe a prophet. The answer was simple: you know by whether or not the message comes true. In Deuteronomy 18:21, 22, Moses writes,

> "And you may say in your heart, 'How shall we know the word which the LORD has not spoken?'

> "When a prophet speaks in the name of the LORD, if the thing does not come about or come true, that is the thing which the LORD has not spoken. The prophet has spoken it presumptuously; you shall not be afraid of him."

Today we are equipped with two additional checks: (1) the presence of the written Word of God in the hands of virtually every believer to serve as the objective standard of evaluation, and (2) the internal witness of the Holy Spirit to discern the spirit of the prophet.

Just because a person utters a prophecy does not automatically make him a prophet, any more than winning a man to Christ necessarily makes the witnessing person an evangelist. But the point still holds: to be a true prophecy, it must align with the Scriptures and come true.

The first prophecy which ever came to my attention was so phony even a rank pagan could have spotted it as absurd! It happened several years ago on the second anniversary of the assassination of Martin Luther King.

Two or three of us were sitting in my living room having fellowship that afternoon, when another brother came to the door to announce a prophetic revelation. He was just about a year old in the Lord and was a college student. He announced to us he had been given a word from the Lord that Dr. King and the late Robert F. Kennedy were the two witnesses mentioned in Revelation 11, and that if we could round up all the believers we knew and get together at a mass meeting before sundown to proclaim them as God's two witnesses, they both would come back from the dead and help spread the Gospel to the world.

I wanted to stand up and preach at him and shake some sense into him. But the Lord suppressed my "fumes" and even took away my initial desire to try to shoot down the brother's "prophecy." I sensed the guidance of the Holy Spirit as I quietly asked my friend to tell me more.

He went through the whole story again, this time in more detail. He finished, paused a moment, and then asked, "What do you think?"

I read, without comment, Paul's warning in I Timothy 4:1:

> But the Spirit explicitly says that in later times some will fall away from the faith, paying attention to deceitful spirits and doctrines of demons.

Then I read Brother Peter's words (II Peter 2:1, 2):

> But false prophets also arose among the people, just as there will also be false teachers among you, who will secretly introduce destructive heresies, even denying the Master who bought them, bringing swift destruction upon themselves.
>
> And many will follow their sensuality, and because of them the way of the truth will be maligned.

Looking up at him from the pages of the Word, I said, "Brother, what you've said is right from the devil."

"Is it really?" he answered. "Well if it is, I'm really glad to know because this thing has been like a monkey on my back ever since it came on me."

"My suggestion," I said, "would be that we all take a minute right now and ask the Lord to deliver you from this deceptive spirit."

It was as though my buddy couldn't pray fast enough! Together we prayed in the name of Jesus Christ, claiming the blood of Christ over the enemy and commanding that Satan be bound. Instantly this young brother was freed from the oppression and, really, the whole event became a major turning point in his spiritual life. From that day

63

forth, he exhibited a solidarity in his walk with Christ and in his understanding of the Word of God he had not known before. He and his wife are serving the Lord with gladness today.

A year or so later, after moving to Memphis, we were part of a group of about two dozen believers gathered together one morning in the home of a Christian couple. While we were in prayer that morning a prophecy came which instantly I knew was from the Lord. In fact, after it was given, the man who spoke it said, "Does anyone witness to that?"

A resounding "Yes!" came from the group.

Tragically, that prophecy came true. Essentially the message given was, "My little children, stay close to Me and to each other, for a false teacher will come in among you and will lead many of you astray."

That was the last time this group ever met. A week later a man arrived on the scene to draw away people after himself, and these people — who were once closest of friends — now found it virtually impossible even to communicate with one another. To this day some are following this self-anointed apostle. I must say, however, that one day the group will be together again, and I believe it will happen on this side!

THE DISTINGUISHING OF SPIRITS

It was Sunday night open house at our home in Memphis, and the believers were present, singing up a storm and praising the Lord for what He had been doing the past week.

While one of the brothers was sharing a passage from the Scriptures, three men walked in the front door. I'd seen one of them before; the other two were strangers. But they appeared to know each other. Some of the kids scooted over on the floor and made room for them to sit down.

The brother who was speaking finished, and the Lord put some more music in our hearts. After two or three songs, someone else stood to thank God for answered prayer.

Then one of the new guys asked to say a word. "I'm new in town," he said, "and I've opened up a halfway house down the street for runaways and heads. I'm not really into Jesus like y'all are — in fact, I don't believe He was the Son of God — but if any of you would like to come down and help out. . . ."

And while he was in the middle of his sentence, a normally quiescent middle-aged brother whose walk with the Lord is a showpiece stood up, pointed his finger at the visitor, and said firmly, "In the name of Jesus Christ, I command you to leave."

Mouths all around the room dropped open. I could not believe what I had heard. For months and months we had met together, praised the Lord, and had been built up in love, and now *this* had to happen. I was utterly speechless. The blood drained out of my head, and I sat there like a toad blinking in a rainstorm.

The stranger went to the front door, opened it, walked out closing the door behind him, and was gone. Nobody said a word.

Finally the son-in-law of the man who had asked the stranger to leave broke the silence. "Dad, what on earth did you do that for?" he asked.

"That man was right out of the pit," he answered.

"How can you say that?" Doug retorted. "Besides, maybe the Lord sent him here to become a Christian."

"All I know is, I got mighty strong signals from the Holy Spirit that he had to go," the older man replied. "And when the Spirit tells me something, I do it."

Doug walked over to the front hallway. "I'm going out to apologize to him," he said as he left the house.

No one knew what to say or do. I respected this older brother so completely that I felt out of place to disagree with him; yet I hated for a spectacle to be made of the visitor. Maybe he *did* come to meet the Lord.

One by one, the younger brothers and sisters began to voice disapproval at what had happened. But the brother held his ground. "I've seen this kind of thing happen before," he assured us. "The devil will send some guy into a place where the saints are gathered and put on a real good, sincere show. But when that man made his open denial of Jesus Christ, my spirit said, 'That's it!'"

This interaction went on for fifteen or twenty minutes. Questions would come, and answers followed. Finally the older brother began to back down.

"Listen," he said. "If none of you witness to what I did, then maybe I was operating in the flesh. All I know is, when the man was speaking I felt a tremendous compulsion that he must go."

The discussion continued. Another few minutes passed by and then Doug returned to the meeting.

"Dad, I owe *you* the apology," he said. "That guy really *was* from the pit. It was clear in talking with him that he had come to recruit some folks and mess them up by talking them out of their faith in Jesus Christ."

Talk about praising the Lord! Everybody was thrilled at how God had looked after us. And it was through a brother who had the guts to exercise his spiritual gift — the gift of the *discernment of spirits* — for the benefit and common good of the whole body.

That night has become a milestone for me. I'll never forget it. I had *never* understood the gift before, or how it could work. I was so thankful to the Lord as the great Shepherd of the sheep, I could not express it.

You know, in many of our Christian meetings, we so completely organize, delegate, and supervise the Holy Spirit out of a job that He could scarcely break through with a word if He wanted to! We've got it all wrapped up. The heavenly head, Jesus, has been forced to give way to human heads, and we miss out.

It is about time we recognize the Lord Jesus as the *experiential head* of the body and not just as the theological head. Oh, we all know that He is Lord. We'd say that in a minute. But letting Him be Lord on paper, or on a gray cornerstone, is not what He's after! He wants to be the real live Lord of His body, of His children, as they come together in His name. And if we will let Him be King, He'll not only lead us, but He'll protect us from evil.

In my travels to various places, and in sharing with the saints in these places, it is obvious God is breaking through along these lines in so many ways. People are becoming more and more open to the creative work of the Holy Spirit. They are trusting Him for corporate leadership, not just for personal leadership. And when this begins to happen on a broad basis, devil look out! When we let Jesus really *direct* His body, rather than be just one of its many activities, why, all heaven will break loose!

When Peter and John came to Samaria in Acts 8, a brand-new believer named Simon, a man who had been heavy into sorcery, came with them. Simon was greatly intrigued at the power and authority of the apostles, especially when they laid hands on the Samaritans to receive the Holy Spirit.

> Now when Simon saw that the Spirit was bestowed through the laying on of the apostles' hands, he offered them money,
>
> saying, "Give this authority to me as well, so that everyone on whom I lay my hands may receive the Holy Spirit."
>
> But Peter said to him, "May your silver perish with you, because you thought you could obtain the gift of God with money!
>
> "You have no part or portion in this matter, for your heart is not right before God."   (Acts 8:18-21)

It was the gift of the discerning of spirits given to Peter which enabled him to understand the bondage to sin in Simon's heart. And Simon repented, for he knew that Peter spoke the truth from God.

This matter of the discernment of spirits happened one more time at our house. It was another Sunday night meeting, and God used the same brother as His "private eye." This time the person asked to leave was a fourteen-year-old girl involved in Satan worship. The brother spotted her, and out she went.

This time *I* was the one who followed her out the door. Though I had no doubt that God wanted her out, I wanted to talk with her for myself and understand her side of the story.

She told me how she had taken a vow to Satan, and that her goal in life was to reign on the earth with him.

"You'll get *rained on*," I told her, referring to the end of Revelation 20.

We sat in my driveway, and for thirty minutes I explained the Gospel to her. She rejected Jesus cold.

As I got up to go back into the house to rejoin the fellowship, I said, "It really is better that you stay away from these meetings. The more you hear the Gospel and turn it down, the harder your heart will become to ever receiving Christ. Also, the presence of Satan in your life throws some pretty bad vibes into the meeting, and your spirit will only hassle the spirits of the Christians in there.

"But if you ever want to know Christ," I told her, "here's my number. You can phone me anytime, day or night. But until that time, it's best for you and for us that you stay away."

She never called. But two years later we were told that she had surrendered her life to Jesus Christ. More and more I've come to understand how the gifts of the Spirit are for the good of the body and are really necessary to its full health.

seven/The Gifts: Tongues and Interpretation

> ...to another various kinds of tongues, and to another the interpretation of tongues. But one and the same Spirit works all these things, distributing to each one individually just as He wills. (I Corinthians 12:10b, 11)

Buckle up, friends, because here we go on the two gifts that qualify as the biggest "Christian friendship and oneness busters" of the century.

In this chapter tongues and the interpretation of tongues will be considered jointly, as Paul suggests repeatedly the utterance of tongues in public is best accompanied by an interpretation which should follow (I Corinthians 14:5, 13, 27, 28).

Opinions Vary

Many teachers say there is a difference between the *gift* of tongues and *speaking* in tongues. One, they say, is the public language and needs interpretation; the other is a private prayer language exercised as a communication between the believer and God, and thus needs no interpretation. The gift of speaking in tongues in public is given to some, they continue, while the prayer language is available to all who have received the gift of the Holy Spirit. In fact, the private language is the outward evidence of having received the gift of the Spirit.

But there are other opinions. One prominent teaching is that tongues vanished from the scene at the close of the first century. A more moderate view is that tongues are possible today, but certainly not a requisite for the Spirit-filled life.

Virtually all biblical scholars agree that tongues were present both when the Holy Spirit was given at Pentecost, and throughout the first century. "And they were all filled with the Holy Spirit and began to speak with other tongues, as the Spirit was giving them utterance" (Acts 2:4). If you can take the word "all" literally in this passage (and I see no reason to suppose that you cannot) then 120 Christians spoke with tongues, including the apostles.

As the ministry of the Holy Spirit expanded geographically to regions beyond, often the first people to receive the Holy Spirit in a given area were also imbued with the gift of tongues (Acts 10:46; 19:6). Tongues are considered in I Corinthians 14 as to their use in the assembly of the believers.

And tongues are back today, live and in color.

The Happy Hustler

I had just finished speaking at a noonday luncheon in a city in Ohio. The purpose of the affair was for believers to bring friends and associates who did not profess Christ to hear the good news of knowing Him as Lord. It was one of those times when I sensed I was particularly anointed of the Spirit to speak the word of life.

After the program was over, three ladies approached me. One, who turned out to be the spokeswoman for the group said, "Young man, have you been baptized with the Holy Spirit?"

"Yes, Ma'am," I said.

"Did you receive the evidence?" she asked.

"Yes, Ma'am, I did."

"Oh, praise God, you have the gift of tongues!" she said, nodding approval to her two friends.

"No, Ma'am, I don't," I responded. "God gave me another gift."

She looked disappointed, almost crestfallen. She waited a few moments, then spoke again.

"Which one did you get?" she asked hesitatingly.

"The gift of evangelism," I said. "I met the Lord in college, and knew that He had come into my life. But the first three months of my Christian life were really fruitless. Though Christ was with me, I still controlled my life. I'd witness to others, and nothing would ever happen. Usually they were alienated by what I said.

"One night I heard a man speak on the ministry of the Holy Spirit. I had never even considered the fact that the Holy Spirit was personal, and could fill and control my life. That night I simply allowed Him to fill me and to *be* my very life. He did, and He has given me a boldness and desire to share the Lord which I never knew before."

I could see she was dissatisfied with my answer. It was as though she wanted to say something; maybe even defend herself, but did not know how to respond.

Finally I said, "Look, how would you feel if right now I were to sit you down in a chair, lay my hands on you, and pray you would get my gift. How would that make you feel?"

She was startled at my suggestion. But she looked back

71

at me and said, "Thank you. I needed someone to tell me that."

Please don't get me wrong. She was a dear, precious sister in Christ. And I enjoyed talking with her and look forward to knowing her for eternity. But do you know what she had planned to do? She wanted to hustle me for tongues. *And there's nowhere in the Bible where people got hustled for tongues!* There are plenty of places where people spoke with tongues, but nowhere were they *hustled* for tongues.

BUT AREN'T MOST OF US HUSTLERS?

I submit that this is what has caused much of the conflict today. We've been out drumming up business for the gifts, rather than ministering the Holy Spirit to one another. And it's not even remotely limited to the "tongues" brethren, either. We all tend to hustle "our" gift or gifts.

The man with the gift of teaching encourages everyone to be a teacher. The evangelist says the key to living the Christian life is winning people to Christ daily. I've even had people with the gift of helps lay the trip on me that unless I spend more time helping my fellow man, I am displeasing to God.

But didn't God say there was to be variety, diversity? He promised us variety right from the start (I Corinthians 12:4-6). And the gifts are given *first* to the church, *not* to the individual. So what business do we have running around trying to get other people into our gifts when God said it is *He* who passes out the gifts?

Those in the body of Christ who possess the manifestation of tongues are seeing the problems which have come through the overemphasis on tongues, too. Not long ago at a Full Gospel meeting in Memphis, the statement was made by a speaker, "If somehow we could take a person who has received the experience of tongues and lock him up for six months, many of our problems would be solved!"

Every year in the late fall Marilyn and I go Christmas shopping for our kids. We try to select presents for them which we feel will be exactly what they want. Our desire is to handpick for each child the items we think he or she will like.

And you know what? It really makes me angry when, on Christmas morning, the kids get up at dark-thirty to open their presents, and they storm into our bedroom and complain, "How come Greg got that, and I only got this?" Or, "Why did Ginger get a doll, and I got a storybook?" I suppose nothing that happens all the rest of the calendar year gets to me more.

Can you imagine how God feels when, after giving gifts to His people, they go out and fight with each other and complain over their distribution? That's *exactly* what is going on. And it's got to stop! Brothers and sisters, this behavior is absolutely childish. It's infantile. And it's a stench in the nostrils of God.

It is not up to us down on this level to disperse the gifts or to name the gift our brother or sister receives. It *is* our business to see that they are members of God's forever family, headed up by the Lord Jesus Christ; but it is not our business to fight and squabble over the gifts, or to reject each other just because our gifts differ.

DIVERSITY — PLUS!

A couple of summers ago I was invited to a conference in the Midwest. Talk about diversity. The saying "Different strokes for different folks" seemed to be the only proper caption for the list of speakers and teachers. But all were right-on, born-again Christians who loved the Lord and His Word.

On the opening evening a brother gave a message on the church as the body of Christ. In his deliberation he compared the make-up of the early church with the church of this age. When he closed his talk, he invited the 200 or so of us who were listening to kneel down by our chairs for a time of intercession for further awakening in the body.

He led off in prayer, and at the close of his petitions he

prayed audibly in an unknown tongue. Another brother, kneeling down close to him, interpreted the tongue. My spirit witnessed to both the utterance and its interpretation, though I understood little of what was happening. Several others prayed, and after fifteen minutes or so, the session ended.

I had no idea how disturbed people were until I saw him literally mobbed by members of the audience. Two college girls came up to me in tears, asking what had transpired. "We don't understand it," they sobbed.

It was after 2:00 A.M. before I was able to get to bed, the questions and concerns were so numerous. The brother who spoke was kept up almost all night by assailants who wanted equal time.

The next morning, before the opening session got officially under way, the speaker of the night before asked to say a few words. *What he said changed me,* because it settled in my heart an attitude I had been searching for within the body of Christ, but had not yet found.

"Many of you," he began, "have forced people like me into an unbiblical position. There is only one place in America that I can freely exercise my spiritual gift, and that is in the tongues movement. And I'm here to say, the tongues movement is unbiblical.

"There is only one movement on earth that God has started for this age, and that movement is the body of Christ. And when He gave gifts to His church, He meant for them to be used in the total body of Christ, and not off to the side somewhere in a freewheeling operation begun and encouraged by men.

"Last night I exercised one of my spiritual gifts. I asked nobody here to acquire that gift. In fact, I couldn't care less if any of you ever acquire it. All I ask is that you give me the privilege and freedom to exercise my gifts, and I will give you the privilege and freedom to exercise yours."

He stomped on my heart. On so many occasions in the

past I had assumed the headship of the body and quelled the expression of the gifts. Not just tongues. A lot of them. And I want to tell you, that morning I repented. I changed my mind, as the Lord revealed an error. My whole attitude began to change toward those with gifts different from my own.

COMING OUT OF THE TUNNEL

I say something at this point that to some will sound very subjective. I have talked with many of the non-tongues crowd of believers who know the overseas missions scene well, who say that the mightiest work God is doing today in South America, is being done through those members of the body of the Pentecostal persuasion.

As I travel and minister in the work God has given me to do, I must say that *generally speaking*, the most excited believers I meet are those who have had the "charismatic experience" (and nobody hates labels more than I do!). Let me quickly add something to that statement. I do not believe for a moment that tongues gives *anyone* a measure of victory not available to all; it is the Holy Spirit who changes our lives. But I am saying that God is doing a very lovely thing in the lives of those who have experienced some of the traditionally "no-no" gifts, and I think it's high time some of the rest of us listen to what they are saying.

For so long I have had "tunnel vision," being one in the Spirit only with those Christians upholding my own doctrinal traditions. At this time, however, the closest Christian friends I have are people who have been reached for Christ through those with the charismatic emphasis. This is the first time I have really made myself vulnerable to people whose gifts are that much different from my own. Both Marilyn and I have grown immensely through this relationship. In a way, I feel cheated because I have never before made room to include people with "charismatic" gifts into my circle of intimates. Shame on me! I've been the loser.

Unity Really Can Happen

All of us will agree that the ultimate program of God is to bring His people together into a oneness in Christ that will be forever. Granted, most feel this oneness will come only after the kingdom is revealed, and I agree. But if oneness is His purpose in eternity, is there any way that division and strife could be His purpose now? Especially when His Word teaches such things as:

> So then you are no longer strangers and aliens, but you are fellow-citizens with the saints, and are of God's household, having been built upon the foundation of the apostles and prophets, Christ Jesus Himself being the cornerstone, in whom the whole building, being fitted together is growing into a holy temple in the Lord; in whom you also are being built together into a dwelling of God in the Spirit. (Ephesians 2:19-22)

> Being diligent to preserve the unity of the Spirit in the bond of peace. There is one body and one Spirit, just as also you were called in one hope of your calling; one Lord, one faith, one baptism, one God and Father of all who is over all and through all and in all. But to each one of us grace was given according to the measure of Christ's gift. (Ephesians 4:3-7)

> And coming to Him as to a living stone, rejected by men, but choice and precious in the sight of God, you also, as living stones, are being built up as a spiritual house for a holy priesthood, to offer up spiritual sacrifices acceptable to God through Jesus Christ.
> (I Peter 2:4, 5)

One more thing: "standing for the truth" today is a really big thing. It was big in the first century; it is big today. But most of us define the truth (don't we?) as essentially *our* position.

I am not for a moment down on rightly dividing the word of truth. But it's the *word of truth* that is the truth, not our *dividing* of it.

Do you expect to check into eternity with a perfect 100 percent on your theology test? I surely don't. I would like to be in the high 90s, but I certainly don't believe my interpretation is flawlessly pristine.

We are not talking here about accepting every Tom, Dick, and Harry who comes along with an ounce or two of spiritual truth, and instantly calling him a brother. Rather, we are dealing with a situation that is taking place *among* brothers. *This is a brother-to-brother, not a brother-to-pagan issue.* One of the sins God hates the most is causing division among brothers (Proverbs 6:16-19). He's just really down on that.

There is a vast and glorious array of brothers and sisters in Christ who are waiting to discover each other, and who, until now, have been afraid to open up to one another because their gifts are different.

eight / Being Baptized in the Holy Spirit

For even as the body is one and yet has many members, and all the members of the body, though they are many, are one body, so also is Christ.

For by one Spirit we were all baptized into one body, whether Jews or Greeks, whether slaves or free, and we were all made to drink of one Spirit.

For the body is not one member, but many.

(I Corinthians 12:12-14)

There are some passages in the Scriptures which, when held up against past and current history, come out almost funny.

For example, remember back in Matthew 6, in the Sermon

on the Mount, when Jesus was teaching His disciples about prayer? He talked first about praying to the Father in secret, because the whole purpose of prayer was to communicate with God, and not to appear as "religious" before men.

And then, in Matthew 6:7, 8, Jesus said in effect, don't say prayers over and over again (with the implication being that faith, not repetition, is the means of getting God's attention). Jesus' words were:

> "And when you are praying, do not use meaningless repetition, as the Gentiles do, for they suppose that they will be heard for their many words.

> "Therefore do not be like them; for your Father knows what you need, before you ask Him."

In the following verse, nine, the Lord Jesus prayed a prayer to illustrate the way His people ought to pray. It was a prayer to show that *repetition* was out and that just plain *conversation* with God was in. Yet what prayer is it that we pray over and over in our meetings? It is the prayer Jesus gave to illustrate the idea of not repeating prayers. We know it today as "The Lord's Prayer," which begins in Matthew 6:9!

THE MEANING OF THE SPIRIT'S BAPTISM

In a similar way, we seem to have missed the point of being baptized with the Holy Spirit. Because the baptism of the Spirit in I Corinthians 12:13 is the one work of the Spirit designed to bring together the vast diversity in the members of the body of Christ. Let's look at the passage again:

> For even as the body is one and yet has many members, and all the members of the body, though they are many, are one body, so also is Christ.

> For by one Spirit we were all baptized into one body, whether Jews or Greeks, whether slaves or free, and we were all made to drink of one Spirit.
>
> (I Corinthians 12:12, 13)

79

Paul's whole argument in those two verses is this: "There are many, many members in the body of Christ, and by one Spirit we were all baptized into that body — whether Jew or Greek (Gentile), slave or free, and we all partake of that same Spirit." Do you see it? The baptism of the Holy Spirit is designed to take people with all sorts of differences and make them *one* in the body of Christ. And the very truth God displayed to make people one is the one we fight over most — being baptized with the Holy Spirit.

FIGHTING THE BAD FIGHT

I remember a certain day in seminary. Lunch hour was almost over, and afternoon classes were ready to begin. There was a commotion in the snack shop, with voices rising high. As a green first-year man, I was shocked to the point of gross disenchantment to poke my nose in at the door and to see and hear brethren screaming and yelling hatefully at each other — over how to experience the Holy Spirit.

How ironical that the very means God set forth to show that we, being many, can be molded into one body in Christ — the baptism of the Spirit — can be so *bitterly* disputed. In Christ we are above this kind of divisive factionalism. By God's grace, I have had my last argument over this issue, and I pray that my readers will hold me to this stance!

LITTLE COUNTRY CHURCH ON THE EDGE OF TOWN

Several years ago I was asked to speak in the evening service at the "showcase" evangelical church in a small town near where we were living. The Lord directed me to speak that night on the work of the Holy Spirit in the lives of believers. At the close of the service I extended an invitation to those who knew they were Christians, but who were not walking in the Spirit, to let the Holy Spirit flood and control their lives. There were many who responded.

I recall that after the gathering the pastor mentioned he admired my "sense of conviction" and the way in which I taught the Word of God in the power of the Spirit. I reiterated it was not my power, but that of the Holy Spirit, which enabled me to speak with authority and conviction.

It was not two or three months later that a phone call came from a fellowship of believers meeting near the location of this church building. These were Christians who were aglow with the Spirit, who were leading others to Christ and seeing specific answers to their prayers. The brother who called reported that this minister had come into the group preaching about the Holy Spirit and had gotten everyone confused.

What had happened was this: the pastor had been filled with the Holy Spirit, had received the gift of tongues, and had told these believers that unless their experience essentially matched his own, there was grave doubt the Holy Spirit could control their lives.

The next morning I got into my car and drove seventy miles to the "scene of the accident."

First, I listened to the Christians in the group. Their concern — and even fear — was obvious. Then I called the pastor (who had been kicked out of his church as soon as the board heard of his experience) and asked to see him. We met in a cafeteria.

I was thrilled to learn of what the Lord had done for him. Here was a man who a few months earlier was a picture of spiritual defeat and who had now come alive in Christ. He was like a drowning man who had been hauled ashore. The trouble was, he had accused the crowd standing on shore helping with his rescue of drowning with him, and they weren't within twenty feet of the water! He told me his overriding concern was that the people in this particular group had not had the opportunity to experience the Holy Spirit. Another Spirit-filled Christian and I had been the primary teachers for the group.

"Do you believe I am baptized in the Holy Spirit?" I asked the brother.

"Yes, I do," the man replied hesitatingly.

"If I were a person who denied the Lord Jesus Christ and

the authority of the Scriptures and the power of the Holy Spirit, you would have every reason to come here and straighten out this group. Or, if I were a Christian operating in the energy of the flesh, you would have reason to take the reins and teach.

"But as it is, you are teaching these people that they are fleshly, and in need of the Holy Spirit, yet they already have the Holy Spirit. Brother, that's dangerous."

Reluctantly he agreed. And he made right the confusion he had caused.

Though there were some jolted spirits that took a few weeks to recover, the Lord was glorified in the whole situation.

You know, many of the problems we are facing today relative to this matter will be solved if only we will *deal* with them, rather than just *preach* about them. The Scriptures say *go* to a brother with whom there is a grievance. Many times we *gossip* instead of *go*, and the whole body suffers as a result.

What Is the Baptism of the Holy Spirit?

Most serious students of the Bible, from the Reformed theologian to the traditional Pentecostal, will agree there are two basic aspects of the work of the Holy Spirit for the believer: Phase I — the work of the Holy Spirit with regard to regeneration (new birth) as explained in John 3:3-6; Phase II — the work of the Holy Spirit for day-to-day living (new walk) as expressed in passages such as Galatians 5:25.

There is general unanimity of opinion on Phase I — the new birth. The disagreement concerns Phase II — the new walk: when it begins, and how it works. As we have already discussed in chapter three, it *is* possible to be born of the Spirit, and yet not walk in the Spirit. So what we are talking about is how to help make sure those who are born anew are experiencing the baptism and filling of the Holy Spirit.

The majority of Pentecostal and charismatic teachers believe that Phase I (the work of the Spirit in the new birth) and Phase II (the baptism of the Spirit leading to the new walk) are usually two different events for the Christian. Most other Bible students believe that the work of the Holy Spirit, Phase I and Phase II, happens at the same time at the new birth and the believer begins then to appropriate or *experience* the fullness of the Holy Spirit.

With the present outpouring of the Holy Spirit across so many lines in the body of Christ, everyone is having to take a second look. Who, for example, can deny the reality of change in the life of a man who, say, made a profession of faith at "First Church" twenty years ago, but who just last week received the baptism of the Spirit and has already led three people to Jesus Christ and has seen God heal his brother-in-law of chronic asthma? And on the other hand, what knowledgeable charismatic would question the reality of the Holy Spirit's baptism and fullness in the life of another Christian who has walked in power with the Lord from the moment of his new birth, praising God, encouraging the saints, loving and giving unashamed witness to the world's people, though perhaps never having uttered a prophecy or spoken with a heavenly tongue?

Let's get a couple of things straight — and I'm going to stop just writing for a moment and start preaching. I'll begin with us evangelicals —

It's about time we started emphasizing the *reality* of the baptism and filling of the Holy Spirit. Let's quit being so concerned with *when* it happened, and instead make sure *that* it happens! I'm so sick and tired of lifeless, sleepy, unmotivated, doctrinally correct, eternally secure orthodox evangelical Christians I want to croak. And you must want to, too. And fellow-shepherds, a lot of it is our fault! We're just not preaching the Spirit's miracles and fullness as we should. And maybe it's because we know little or nothing of it ourselves.

We've prayed for years, "Lord, let us see again that which happened in the Book of Acts. Do it again, Lord." Well, we'd better wake up because it's happening, and a lot of us know it's happening but we're too chicken to admit it. Our charismatic brethren are experiencing a lot of what went on in the first century. Sure, they've got their problems, too. But let's quit hiding behind their inconsistencies for a moment and realize that God has His hand on some lovely people called "charismatics."

One of our favorite theme-song verses in evangelicalism is "Faith cometh by hearing, and hearing by the word of God" (Romans 10:17 KJV). We've used that verse, and rightly so, for getting out and preaching the truth of salvation in Jesus Christ. It's a plain fact: it's tough to *believe* God unless you *hear* Him speak.

People today — Christians — need to *hear* about the Holy Spirit. Then they need to *believe* the baptism and fullness of the Holy Spirit. Having it as "positional truth," my brothers and sisters, is *not getting the job done!* We can have positional truth coming out our ears, but what we need at this hour is the Book-of-Acts *reality* of the Holy Spirit in our lives.

And speaking of the Book of Acts, here is what I've started doing. (If this bothers some, let me say it has biblical precedent and it works!) When a person I share the Gospel with places his faith in Christ, if at all possible, I lay hands on him right there and ask the Lord that moment to immerse him in, and fill him with, the Holy Spirit. Then I say to that person something like, "Brother (or Sister), right now by faith, receive the Holy Spirit." And in child-like faith, a brand-new believer can receive the Spirit in His fullness, and not have to spend years and years in defeat.

This is the *norm!* God never meant for a believer in Christ to spend years in left field spiritually. Let's share the reality of the Holy Spirit on the front end as they did in the New Testament era.

And one more word to us evangelicals. Quit crawling all over the charismatics. Granted, there have been mistakes and excesses among charismatics. But there are carloads of people walking in the Spirit and praising the Lord because of what they've found through the charismatic ministry. And a lot of people have been just plain saved, too.

Now, I want to preach at us charismatics for a bit. And I say *us* charismatics, because I'm one, too. Don't you tell me that I'm not charismatic just because I've never manifested tongues. I'm baptized in the Spirit, filled with the Spirit, and possess several gifts of the Spirit; therefore, I'm charismatic.

Charismatics, we need to do more of what the evangelicals have been doing while they've neglected talking about the baptism. We need to do a whale of a lot more exhortation on *walking* in the Spirit. Who cares if ol' Joe got the baptism of the Spirit with every tongue available back in the Spring of '02, if he's not walking in the Spirit right now?

I've met far too many believers who've received the baptism of the Spirit who are as carnal as bedbugs in the way they live. Some are on a bad "the end justifies the means" kick, claiming they have the authority to pull off things contrary to the Scriptures because they have God's power in them and He told them to do it. That's cheatin'.

Brothers and sisters, the baptism in the Spirit is *not* the big deal. It's the all-important *beginning* of the big deal, but it's not the end in itself. The big deal is walking in the Spirit moment by moment, day by day. Experiencing His present leading and control.

One other word to us charismatics. Quit pressuring other Christians who are already filled with the Holy Spirit. Some of the brethren who have received the manifestation of tongues have made a sterile religion out of it. Praise the Lord if He has given you the utterance. But don't let the manifestation of tongues become Lord of your life. There is only one Lord, and I doubt if anyone or anything else will ever step up and take His place. Just because another brother or sister is not bilingual has little or nothing to do with his or her love for Christ or power with God. Phase out of the mentality which says, "If you don't speak with tongues, you're not Spirit-filled." Corinth had every spiritual gift on the list when they took their first-century flesh trip.

There's a difference between shoving people into the Spirit and leading them into the Spirit. If you are alive in the Holy Ghost, the sweet aroma of the fragrance of Christ in your life will be more than adequate to attract others to know Him in a deeper way. If the living water flows from your being, many will come by on a regular basis to have a drink with you. You won't need to squirt them in the face!

So, what is the baptism of the Holy Spirit? As was noted earlier, to be baptized means to be placed into, immersed, identified with. The baptism of the Spirit is that majestic inundation of the child of God by the glorious Third Person of the Trinity. It's where your life becomes His; your will submits while His Spirit reigns.

And in First Corinthians 12:13 we read, "For by one Spirit we were all baptized into one body, . . . and we were all made to drink of one Spirit." That is where the Holy Spirit takes all believers — even those who are arguing over what the baptism of the Holy Spirit really means — and places them into one body, Christ's, where hopefully they can quit arguing and begin enjoying the Lord and one another!

THE REAL ISSUE

A friend of mine tells a beautiful story, which is not original with him. We've searched, but neither of us can find the true source, so allow me the liberty of passing it on, giving the Lord the credit. The truth it sets forth is incomparable.

It's late in the second year of Jesus' public ministry, and He is teaching a group of His followers on a Judean hillside. Among those in the crowd are two men who have not met before and who happen to be seated next to each other.

While the Lord is revealing the things of God to the throng, the one man nudges the other and remarks, "Isn't He wonderful?"

"He certainly is," whispers the second. "He healed me of blindness, you know."

"He did!" says the first with surprise. "He healed *me* of blindness, too!"

"That's amazing," the second man remarks, motioning to his new friend to pull away from the crowd a bit so their talking will not cause disturbance. "How did it happen?"

"Well, this friend of mine — who was also blind — and I were sitting by the edge of the road just outside of Jericho. We could tell from the voices of an approaching crowd that the Lord was coming our way and would soon pass us on the road.

"When He was within earshot, we yelled up to Him something like, 'Oh Lord, Son of David, give us Your mercy.'

"Jesus called over to us and said, 'What do you want Me to do for you?'

"We said, 'Lord, we just want to be able to see.' And in a flash, we both had our eyesight restored."

"Wait a minute!" says the second man, with a note of contempt in his voice. "There's no way it could have happened like that."

"What are you talking about?" replies the first.

"You've got to have *mud*," says the other. "See, first you spit into your hands, then you stoop down and get some dirt, and go to a pool and wash the mud from your...."

And there you have it, folks. The start of the world's first two denominations. The Mudites and the Anti-Mudites.

Children of God, His new creation has no useful purpose in standing divided, fighting over the gifts, arguing over experiences, trying to make each other do it "our" way, while the world laughs proudly as the devil eggs us on.

nine/ A Place for Us

If the foot should say, "Because I am not a hand, I am not a part of the body," it is not for this reason any the less a part of the body. And if the ear should say, "Because I am not an eye, I am not a part of the body," it is not for this reason any the less a part of the body. If the whole body were an eye, where would the hearing be? If the whole were hearing, where would the sense of smell be?

But now God has placed the members, each one of them, in the body, just as He desired. And if they were all one member, where would the body be? But now there are many members, but one body. And the eye cannot say to the hand, "I have no need of you"; or again the head to the feet, "I have no need of you."
(I Corinthians 12:15-21)

A primary ministry of the Holy Spirit, as we have seen, is to take a variety of believers in Christ Jesus and put them together into one working unit. This unit is made up of people with different spiritual gifts, different ministries, and those whose lives produce different results. This working unit of differing Christians is known as the body of Jesus Christ.

It's Where I Find Myself

Being a part of this body in no way means that each member loses his unique personality and becomes like everyone else. Really, just the opposite is true. The miracle of the whole matter is when the Holy Spirit takes people who are different and fits them in next to other people who also are different and makes them *fit together*. No two pieces of a jigsaw puzzle are the same. Yet when the puzzle is put together properly all the pieces fit. So it is with the body of Christ.

And the Lord is so wise as to where He puts us. As a habit of life, I have often tried to pick and choose the bricks to surround me in God's spiritual building. There were bricks that seemed so comfortable and right to be adjacent to me. But such construction is not usually God's blueprint. For often, as it is no doubt true with you, God has chosen to put me in with bricks that rub and chafe on me a bit. And He does so because He loves me and wants me to be molded and shaped and functioning. "Iron sharpens iron, so one man sharpens another" (Proverbs 27:17). Or, as one friend expresses it, you can choose your friends but you can't choose your family!

"Hey, Frank"

What better illustration of God's people working together as a unit, than for the scriptures to call it "the body" of Christ. For Paul compares the functioning of God's people to the working of a human body. There are arms, legs, feet, hands, eyes, ears, and all the parts. Each part has its own function, and its own purpose. It is attached to the body, not just for its own fulfillment, but for the good of the body as a whole. And when the body is working properly, Jesus Christ actually becomes visible.

If I have a friend named Frank Smith, and see him downtown one day, I do not say, "Hey, there goes Frank Smith's body." I say, "There goes Frank Smith," because Frank is very present within his body. There is no reason in the world for me to separate his personality from his physical body. And the same can be said of the body of Christ. Jesus is not separate from His body; He is very much alive inside it. And when it functions as it ought, people can observe it and see Jesus Christ.

KEEPING THE BODY IN SHAPE

The functioning of this body is a marvelous thing. As a new believer I began by trying to perform every function myself. I was convinced I could do things faster — and maybe better — than most of my brothers and sisters. But, you know, as I've grown in the Lord I have found that I can trust other members to carry out their functions.

Recently word came that a lady who lived nearby had been deserted by her husband. He had been gone for a couple of months and had provided nothing monetarily for her and their children to live on. The local utility company, I learned, had threatened to cut off the gas to the home unless a bill amounting to some $180 was paid at once. Christians in the neighborhood began passing the hat to meet her need. The money was raised before the "hat" ever got to our end of the block.

A day or two later I was conversing with a brother of good financial means who had recently been filled with the Holy Spirit. "Two years ago," he said, "I'd have given the entire $180 myself. But guess how much I gave?"

"How much?" I responded.

"Ten dollars," he said. "The Lord has really been dealing with me about trying to meet people's material needs all

90

alone. And what I've been doing is robbing other brothers from the blessing of giving."

My Spirit witnessed so strongly with his. For I had done exactly the same thing in the area ministering spiritually to others. I was so overly zealous, I would try to have ministry in your life whether the Holy Spirit was leading or not.

God has not only placed the *gifts* in the body just as He has desired, but He puts the *members*, the people, there according to His plan, too. If I am an arm, it is not my business to try to be an eye. Nor should I feel left out because I can't "see" everything as the eye can. God has so composed the body that we can rely on others to function with unique efficiency.

Paul's comment in verse seventeen of I Corinthians 12 is, "If the whole body were an eye, where would the hearing be? If the whole were hearing, where would the sense of smell be?" A great problem today is that the whole body tends to be a *mouth*. How unfortunate that most of the time we as Christians gather together *just to hear a speaker*. Certainly there are speaking gifts: evangelism is one, teaching is another. But there is so much more to the body of Christ than the mouth.

The church has been compared by someone to an NFL football game at which you have 80,000 people who desperately need exercise watching twenty-two men who desperately need rest. Deliver us from being content to permit only a few members of Christ's body to function.

Look Who Needs You!

"The eye cannot say to the hand, 'I have no need of you'; or again the head to the feet, 'I have no need of you'" (I Corinthians 12:21). Not only do the members of the body need one another, but God says that the *head* needs the *members*. And the head is Jesus Christ.

We've often been told that we need Christ, and that is absolutely, eternally true. But do you realize that Christ needs you also? That's what He says. If He hadn't needed

91

you, He would not have called you to be a part of His body.

This is not to imply that God is not all-sufficient in Himself. But in His absolute sufficiency He has chosen to need us. We are precious and valuable to Him. And He seeks for us to worship Him (John 4:23).

I think sometimes we as Christians develop a very low view of ourselves and our magnificent inherent worth in God's sight. Listen! If God didn't think we were worth His rescue, He would never have sent His Son to release His life's blood for us at the cross. We who are the redeemed of God are as a rare jewel, treasured and precious in His sight. If you have been called forth as a member of Christ, remember *God really loves you. Jesus Christ needs you.* You have never been and never will be excess baggage to Him. He purposes to use all that you are in His new creation to the praise of His glory.

TYING IT DOWN

There is one step beyond almost everything said thus far. *Why* does the Spirit lead us? *Why* is Christ to be head of the church? *Why* does God make us fit in the body? *Why* is there a variety of gifts and ministries of the Spirit? *Why* should all the members function?

When Jesus Christ ascended into heaven, His earthly ministry being complete, He left behind the promise of the Holy Spirit (Acts 1:4-8). His prophecy was fulfilled on the day of Pentecost, and the church was born. It all started in Jerusalem, and then spread over the ensuing years throughout Asia Minor and beyond.

Those early churches which sprang up were not just haphazard little groups that somehow accidentally came into existence one fine spring day. They were there, originated by God in His predetermined will, to show forth a life-style of heavenly activities which reflected the Lord; one which the people could know and feel and experience. The apostles had gone forth preaching the Kingdom of God. They publicly displayed Jesus Christ as Lord of Lords and King of Kings — the ruler of that kingdom and the only door by which to enter. They talked about the Cross as the means by which God tore down the barriers keeping people from His kingdom, and the resurrection as proof that there was more to come for those in God's family.

But the work of the apostles did not end with the preaching of the kingdom. As soon as their message was proclaimed, or even coincidentally with that proclamation, a church was established where those who believed the message could begin now to taste of heavenly things. The churches were live models on earth of what was happening in heaven. Eternal life was personal — it had *already* begun — and that life was experienced in the church.

Jesus Christ was present with His people. He was real to them because His Holy Spirit was there. Paul discusses this very thing when he says, "But to each one of us grace was given according to the measure of Christ's gift. Therefore, it says, 'When He ascended on high, He led captive a host of captives, and He gave gifts to men'" (Ephesians 4:7, 8). It was through the diverse gifts of the Spirit that the very living presence of God was made known in the church. The gifts of the Spirit are instrumental in the very rule of the King! Jesus is not yet revealed as King over all the earth; every knee has not yet bowed to Him. But each expression of the body of Christ, each God-governed place, each local assembly of saints does bow to Him and confess Him now as Lord.

The church is where His lordship, His government if you will, can now be known and followed. That term "Lord" is not some convenient proper noun used as a simple synonym for Jesus Christ. It is the active, real acknowledgment of Jesus Christ as experiential *King*. His lordship is meant to be specifically and tangibly known under His governmental authority in the church. Where else would you expect to find a Lord lording or a King ruling other than in his own sphere of government? We are members of His body, citizens of His realm.

93

Do you see why believing God for *all* that He offers is so absolutely crucial? If the Scriptures could be called the constitution of His government, then copping out on ratified provisions is unconstitutional! He desires to rule in fullness and in depth.

The gifts of the Spirit are absolutely vital to the proper functioning of the government of God. They help provide the real life of the eternally true doctrines of our divine magna charta. And, as an aside, the operation of the Spirit's gifts surely helps restrain the world from yelling "bull" at out precious constitution, too! God's gifts bring supernatural balance of spiritual life to God's people.

Can you understand why the gifts of the Spirit have scared some of our Christian leadership to death? Godly men have watched these gifts operate *apart from* the government of God. They have seen the eye say to the hand, "I have no need of you." The body has *not* been coordinated from on high. Thus Paul was forced to say in the first century what he most likely would have to say to our century, "Let all things be done properly and in an orderly manner" (I Corinthians 14:40).

ten /People Who Need People

On the contrary, it is much truer that the members of the body which seem to be weaker are necessary; and those members of the body, which we deem less honorable, on these we bestow more abundant honor, and our unseemly members come to have more abundant seemliness, whereas our seemly members have no need of it. But God has so composed the body, giving more abundant honor to that member which lacked, that there should be no division in the body, but that the members should have the same care for one another.

And if one member suffers, all the members suffer with it; if one member is honored, all the members rejoice with it. Now you are Christ's body, and individually members of it.   (I Corinthians 12:22-27)

In society it is the strong, the articulate, the educated

who keep the system moving. A businessman, for example, is foolish to hire an unlearned man to occupy a key executive role in his firm. And that is as it should be.

But in the body of Christ, the *weaker* people are actually more important than the stronger people. Paul writes that "the members of the body which seem to be weaker are necessary; and those members of the body, which we deem less honorable, on these we bestow more abundant honor..." (I Corinthians 12:22, 23).

The Weak Get Stronger, the Strong Get Weaker

This is not to say we should aim to be weak in the Spirit, and weak in our trust of Jesus Christ. For that same apostle encourages us to "be strong in the Lord, and in the strength of His might" (Ephesians 6:10). Rather, he is talking here about living by God's power, letting His strength be made complete through our weakness (II Corinthians 12:9). Those who are weak in the world's terms, weak according to the flesh, are sponsored by God to be the stabilizers in the church. This explains what Jesus meant when He said, "But the greatest among you shall be your servant" (Matthew 23:11).

In the world, then, the guy with the deep voice, the big frame, the college degree, the authoritative manner — who looks like he just stepped off the front cover of *Gentleman's Quarterly* — this is the man most likely destined for the top. In the body of Christ, however, this gent has a built-in problem, and it is this: he has learned to function for so long a time on his slickness that it is difficult for him to melt in with the common people in the body of Christ. He comes on strong in the flesh and causes trouble. Brothers weak in the flesh, who count on the Holy Spirit instead of themselves as their strength, will be the mainstay of God's people.

This is why God gives "more abundant honor to that member which lacked, that there should be no division in the body, but that the members should have the same care for one another" (I Corinthians 12:24, 25). It's not that God *loves* the weak guy more than the strong. The difference is He can *use* the weaker man more than He can the stronger, because there is less flesh to get in the way — until, of course, the strong man gets weak!

THE GOLDEN OLDIES AND THE YOUNG TURKS

God's preassembled check and balance method for unity in the body is that the weak take on strength, and the strong take on weakness. But there is another natural means of oneness and order in the Lord's people, and this has to do with the principle of older believers, or elders, providing a stable atmosphere for the young in which to grow. Besides His work on patching up divisions that have come over spiritual gifts, I note the Lord to be very busy smoothing out relationships between older, "straight" people and the younger, more individualistic Christians.

Often an older believer will feel the "Jesus Freak" to be operating on a zeal without knowledge, and many times that older Christian is exactly right. Similarly, young believers sense that the older generation in the faith has lost much of its zip — they've been Christians too long for their own good.

But when the body of Christ is really functioning, both are absolutely necessary. Listen! If we could see the combination of the *fire* of the young and the *stability* of the old in operation at this precise point in history, the church would be a real force for principalities and powers to reckon with! Let no man deceive us. We *really* need each other. Both ends of the age spectrum are essential to the proper working of the body.

I'll never forget the night a young, unbelieving college student wandered into a gathering of saints where I was present, in search for the reality of Christ. He had long hair and wore peace-symbol patches on his faded jeans. He sat down next to his exact opposite — a middle-aged IBM executive, an officer in the Naval Reserve — decked out in a fine dark suit which helped to accent his beautiful head of *short*, prematurely gray hair.

Sometime during the meeting, the college kid trusted Christ as his Savior. By the time everyone was ready to go home, the student (who had announced to the group "something had happened" to him during the meeting) turned to the older man and said, "Would you come home with me?"

The older brother was a compassionate, open, Spirit-filled Christian. He had no idea what the younger man had in mind. But what else could he say but "Yes!"

When the two of them reached the younger man's parents' home, the student went in the house and got his flashlight. Then, in the garage, he found a shovel. The older brother held the light, while the younger brother dug up hundreds of dollars worth of amphetamines which he had buried in the backyard. A few minutes later, the parents watched in utter disbelief while their son methodically flushed the stash down the garbage disposal in the kitchen. People had suspected he was a user; no one dreamed he was a dealer.

It was significant to me that this new believer turned to one with whom he could identify, not in the flesh but in the Spirit, to be his back-up man as he cut the ties with his past. And it was through the loving counsel of the older brother later that evening that the young brother took his first solid steps of growth with Jesus Christ.

THE COMPANY OF THE COMMITTED

Theologian Elton Trueblood has referred to God's people as "the company of the committed." It is incredibly easy to be committed to someone you love. At this stage in history, when human institutions — and even the visible church — have tended toward icy impersonalness, people have needed to sense love and trust before they dared make commitments to each other.

But in the early years of the church, people seemed to *begin* their relationships with commitment, while love and trust developed within that commitment. God's presence was so real to them when they gathered as the church that submission to Him and to His people was not vague as it often is today. They *saw* Him at work in their midst.

I remember a high school history class when we studied ancient cultures where parents chose marriage partners for their children. We kids would shoot strange glances across the room at each other and smirkingly ask in our wordless language, "How on earth could *that* have worked?" Unquestionably those marriages were begun with commitment under parental government, and evidently the vast majority of them made it.

Whenever commitment comes in a relationship, it's *got* to come, or the relationship will eventually fold. On many college campuses today it's really "in" for a guy and gal to decide to live together. People like the idea of being free. But when a couple are living together without commitment, they split when they encounter a difficult obstacle in their personal relationship. A married couple, legally and morally committed to each other, will tend to make it through their obstacles in much stronger fashion because it is more than sexual and emotional compassion which holds them together.

It will be interesting to watch the future development of the thousands upon thousands of "small groups" meeting across this country for worship, prayer, and study. A great number of these groups came into being because the people involved found their spiritual appetites unsatisfied in larger institutional frameworks. I cannot help but predict that either these groups will ultimately fold, or else the people within them will come to a deep commitment and submission to one another whereby the groups will actually become honest-to-goodness churches.

Many people in small groups came together because the freedom they desired in their big churches did not exist. In their small group experiences they may have found just what they wanted: *freedom*. But freedom isn't good enough.

It won't hold the group together. It's back to that common-law marriage thing again. Somewhere, there will need to come commitment and order, or it will fold.

It goes back to God's government expressed in the church. Ultimately He's after order and authority. By this I am not suggesting rigidity and dictatorial reign. I'm talking about 2,000-year-old concepts like overseers, elders, shepherds. Whether the labels, as such, exist isn't really all that important. But somehow God is going to gather together Spirit-filled men of tender authority through whom He will lead the sheep of His various folds. "Board action" won't do under this set-up. We're talking about men led of God. Political expedience and Robert's Rules of Order have not done the trick.

PUT THEM ALL TOGETHER, THEY SPELL M-O-T-H-E-R

There's one more aspect to the need we have for each other as members of Christ which I want to mention.

At a gathering of brothers not many months back, a close friend was relating the deep need which was exposed in his own life resulting from the death of his mother while he was still young. He told how that many times the assurance of his father, or the strength of his older brother, was just not enough. He needed a mother, a soft shoulder he could cry on, a personal warmth which only she possessed. For the first time in his life, this element in his family was missing. No one else could replace mother.

He went on to say that sometimes it has been this way in his walk with Christ. Jesus is the firstborn among many brothers, He is our elder brother, and He is strong. He is absolutely imperative in our relationship with God. But there are times when we want to cry on someone's shoulder and be comforted and held close, and we want a mother. Jesus Christ is not a mother; He is our older brother.

We have a father, God the Father. He is all authority and can give us great assurance. There is no one we would ever have, or ever could have, as our Father. But sometimes our need is for a real, live mother.

Then it dawned on my friend. There *is* a mother! It is the bride of Christ, the wife of the Lamb. It is the extension down into time of the heavenly Jerusalem, the city of God; "she is our mother" (Galatians 4:26). *It is the church!* We, corporately, are that mother. We, as brothers and sisters in the Lord Jesus, are the ones with the shoulder to cry on when somebody hurts. We are that soft, warm body which believers need, which *I* need, when I really hurt.

In these painful moments, when a brother or sister is in desperate need, even the gifts I possess are not important. My ministry is not important. The things God has done through me in the past just don't matter. For my brother who is hurting needs none of these things. He needs only a mom.

Have you ever come crying to your mother, pouring out your heart, and end up with her crying too? Or did you ever win a track meet, or earn an A-plus on your term paper, and find that she was just as thrilled, or maybe even more thrilled, than you were? *That's* a mother.

"And if one member suffers, all the members suffer with it; if one member is honored, all the members rejoice with it" (I Corinthians 12:26). Have you ever been around when that's happened? Well, *that's* the church!

eleven / I'm Encouraged!

And God has appointed in the church, first apostles, second prophets, third teachers, then miracles, then gifts of healings, helps, administrations, various kinds of tongues.

All are not apostles, are they? All are not prophets, are they? All are not teachers, are they? All are not workers of miracles, are they?

All do not have gifts of healings, do they? All do not speak with tongues, do they? All do not interpret, do they?

But earnestly desire the greater gifts. And I show you a still more excellent way.   (I Corinthians 12:28-31)

A lady came up to me after I had taught First Corinthians

chapter twelve in a meeting and said, "I don't think I have any spiritual gifts."

"Let's read through the list and see," I suggested.

When we got to the gift of helps, she stopped me and asked, "What was that gift?"

"The gift of helps," I said.

"What does that mean?" she asked.

"Just what it says," I answered. "It means having the spiritual propensity to help people, to do things for others in the body of Christ."

"That's it, that's my gift!" she shouted with delight. "I love to help people, and I do it all the time, but I had no idea it was a spiritual gift."

The implication of the entire twelfth chapter of First Corinthians is that everyone has at least one spiritual gift, no one has them all, and no single gift is possessed by all.

EXPERIENCING YOUR GIFT(S)

With the renewed interest in spiritual gifts today, many believers are asking, "How can I know my gift?" Without going into great detail on the subject, my response is, "What is it, as a Spirit-filled believer, that you feel at home doing and really enjoy doing as a member of the body of Christ?" That's one clue.

Another way of knowing your gifts is through the observations of other Christians. Auditions are held in theater work so that actors can try out for special parts. The director selects those who he feels best fill those spots. In football, spring practice is the time when the coaching staff evaluates which players handle which positions. As the body of Christ "works out," it becomes apparent which believers have gifts of teaching, prophecy, wisdom, faith and all the rest.

The kid who sits in the locker room memorizing plays and reviewing the chalk talk of the past will never really know his capabilities until he gets out onto the field and begins to hit. The actor who does nothing more than learn his lines or apply his make-up will be disappointed when the parts are passed out.

To me, the real issue is not to ask the question, "What is my gift?" The Lord will make that matter clear in His best time. As a member of the body of Christ it is my place, rather, to be available to Him and to others in the body under the leadership of Christ the Head. As this happens, the gifts, the ministries and the results will be clearly manifested through the Holy Spirit.

THERE'S SOMETHING BETTER THAN GIFTS

The Lord, in His wisdom, had a special reason for not giving you or me all His gifts. You see, if each one of us possessed all the gifts, we would have no need for the other. We would all be islands unto ourselves — self-sufficient units with the capability of operational independence.

Paul exhorts us to sincerely desire the gifts of the Spirit, but he says there is something still better. And that which is better is so basic we often miss it. Oh, we see it theologically, but we miss it in practice. He writes,

> If I speak with the tongues of men and of angels, but do not have love, I have become a noisy gong or a clanging cymbal.
>
> And if I have the gift of prophecy, and know all mysteries and all knowledge; and if I have all faith, so as to remove mountains, but do not have love, I am nothing.
>
> And if I give all my possessions to feed the poor, and if I deliver my body to be burned, but do not have love, it profits me nothing.   (I Corinthians 13:1-3)

First Corinthians thirteen is a powerful chaper on love, but it becomes even stronger when we see the *context* in which it is written! The problem in Corinth to which "the love chapter" was addressed was a gifts problem. It is the same basic dilemma we face today. And Paul is asking us — *all* of us — to put love for our brothers and sisters ahead of getting them into our gifts slot.

LET'S GET PERSONAL

Paul says that if I speak with every tongue there is,
known and unknown, and don't love my brothers in Christ —
even those without my gift — and accept them and trust
them in the Holy Spirit just the way they are, then I'm
merely filling the air with noise. (And I've had that attitude, except in reverse. I didn't speak with tongues and
thought everyone who did was something less than I was,
and my attitude *stunk!*)

If I can utter prophecy, and know all about God's eternal
purpose, and have a knowledge of the things of God enough
to teach the Bible like it's going out of style, but don't have
love for all my brothers in Christ — even those who aren't
heavy "Bible people" — then I'm nothing. I'm like a circle
with the edges rubbed off!

And if I'm into social action, and give food and money
to poor people (and heaven knows we need more believers
who do), but don't have love — especially for those who just
preach the Word — then I've missed it all.

Brothers and sisters, I NEED YOU! I can't make it on
my own anymore, because apart from you I am not complete. Jesus Christ is my Savior and my Lord. I am baptized
with the Spirit and filled with the Spirit. If it *had* to be,
that would be enough. But it doesn't have to be, and thus
it isn't enough. If it were enough, God would never have
inaugurated a *body* of believers.

First Corinthians thirteen is crucial because love is the
glue that fastens the body of Christ together. The "charismatic gifts" are great, but if that's all there was, the body
would still be a shambles. The "evangelical gifts" are fine,
but if that's all there were, where would the miraculous
be? The "do-gooder" gifts are beautiful, but if all of us were
social action people, where would the body be?

Picture the body of Christ as being together in a great
big room. Remember back to the "sock-hop" days of the
Fifties when you were in junior high school? All the boys
got together on one side of the gym and all the girls on

the other. A similar thing has happened in the church, only far worse. All the Bible teachers get together over in one corner, all the "soul-winners" in another corner, all the tongues people in a third corner, and the social action Christians in the remaining corner.

God is saying, "Hey! Hey, you Christians. My thought is that if all of you were to bury your special emphases as being qualifications for acceptance and then come together, maybe we could get on with what this business of being the body of Jesus Christ is all about."

This spiritual-segregationist attitude has been quenching the work of the Holy Spirit. We have said, "If we could just get people to see that our ministry or our gift is the key, the job would get done." God says, "If you will just let My Son be the Head, and accept others in the body for what I have made of them, this thing will really work."

During His earthly ministry the Lord Jesus Christ said, "I am the way, and the truth, and the life" (John 14:6). That verse has always been a favorite of mine in seeking to point unbelievers to Christ. Then one day it dawned on me that this passage also has great ramifications for people who are *already* believers. And it has special relevance to the topic at hand.

THE WAY

Jesus is the *way*. He is the way to God, the only way. No one comes to God except through Him. His friends, after His departure from the earth, were referred to as being part of "the Way" (Acts 9:2).

But sometimes we tend to see Jesus *only* as the way, and nothing more. Our whole thrust is to get people into the way, and then the moment we do, to leave them to get more people into the way. In some churches, the way is essentially all that is ever presented — with every Sunday being "decision time" with personal salvation as the theme. The result is that some of the people really know the Lord, but at level number one discipleship. The *way* becomes the whole deal.

THE TRUTH

Jesus is the *truth*. He is the truth concerning God, and He told the truth about God. He sent His Holy Spirit to lead His followers into the truth (John 16:13). The result is that we had men in the first century who obeyed that truth, and men through whom the letters of the New Testament were penned. His Word is truth.

And some of us are into predominantly *truth* trips. Our major emphasis is upon the truth of God. So we, rightly, get people into the Word of God and teach them to divide it correctly (II Timothy 2:15). Our thesis is that if we can just get folks grounded in the Scriptures, they will be solid in the Lord.

THE LIFE

Jesus is the *life*. Without the life there's no living. His Holy Spirit provides life within us, the very life of God.

Many of us are really tuned into the Lord's life, the life of His Holy Spirit inside us. In fact, if the life of the Holy Spirit isn't the central focus of the gathering, we wonder if we haven't wasted our time in coming. Because we have lived in the mildewed atmosphere of dead orthodoxy, and now we hunger for the reality of the life-giving Spirit. And who would argue with this? Our tendency may be to focus on experience, but we've chewed on raw doctrine long enough. What we want is something alive. And our shouts of praise go all the way to heaven and halfway back.

BUT HAVE YOU TRIED THE SUM TOTAL?

Can you imagine the power and reality of the gathered body of Jesus Christ when all this comes together? When it happens, the people of God will have taken their promised dominion on this earth. The overthrow of the planet will be imminent! The firstfruits of this togetherness are already beginning to blossom.

107

Think of all the "way" people that you know. Aren't they really gifted in their proclamation of Jesus as Lord to the unbelieving world? And what about the "truth" folks? Has an era ever known such a vast array of exciting and communicative teachers of the Word of God as ours does? And the "life" crowd — can you think of anything that thrills you more than people *alive* in Jesus Christ?

Now picture these differences in emphasis coming together in a spiritual "media-mix." Can you see it? Here's the "way" people submitting to the total body of Christ and being deepened in the Scriptures and turned on to all the Holy Spirit is doing. Here're the "truth" boys, getting the vision to come outside the cloistered walls to reach a person they could never communicate with before, and to lead him to Christ, and to begin to praise the Lord in the power of the Spirit with spontaneous freshness and joy. Here's the "life" gang, getting ahold of some solid biblical doctrine and becoming real enough to admit that they really do have some emotional lows after all.

The body of Christ has begun discovering itself! It's happening, it really is. And it's going to continue to happen.

Of course, someday when the kingdom of God has fully come, our oneness will be here to stay, and it will be glorious. But why hold out until the end? Let's get on with it now — and avoid a last-minute rush!